Praise for *The Enneagram Guide to Waking Up*

"An outstanding book that offers precise steps to take to wake up to the self-limiting habits of your personality, get out of your own way, and give yourself the gift of accessing more of your higher—more authentic—self."

—**Ian Morgan Cron**, author of *The Road Back to You: An Enneagram Journey to Self-Discovery*

"While there are many new books and podcasts about the Enneagram these days, most of them simply describe the nine types—sometimes in amusing ways, but often as simple stereotypes. It takes many years to really master this material, and Beatrice Chestnut and Uranio Paes have done so. In *The Enneagram Guide to Waking Up*, they not only provide lucid descriptions of the types but also guide the reader beyond this to an understanding of the original purpose of the Enneagram work. They offer wonderful, clear insights and practices that will help you find your dominant type as well as the crucial teachings of what to do with this knowledge. They present accessible methods for transforming your life and 'waking up' as the title suggests. Beatrice and Uranio are true leaders and pioneers in the field of Enneagram studies, and I highly recommend this book to those seeking a deeper understanding of these powerful teachings."

—**Russ Hudson**, author of the audiobook *The Enneagram: Nine Gateways to Presence*, and coauthor of *The Wisdom of the Enneagram*

The
Enneagram
Guide to Waking Up

The
Enneagram
Guide to Waking Up

Find Your Path, Face Your Shadow, Discover Your True Self

BEATRICE CHESTNUT, PHD • URANIO PAES, MM

Foreword by Daniel J. Siegel, MD

HAMPTON ROADS

Cover and text design by Kathryn Sky-Peck
Interior images by Chestnut Paes Enneagram Academy
Typeset in Arno Pro

Hampton Roads Publishing Company, Inc.
Charlottesville, VA 22906
Distributed by Red Wheel/Weiser, LLC

WWW.REDWHEELWEISER.COM
Sign up for our newsletter and special offers by going to *www.redwheelweiser.com/newsletter.*

ISBN: 978-1-64297-031-9
Library of Congress Cataloging-in-Publication Data available upon request.

Printed in the United States of America
IBI

10 9 8 7 6 5 4 3 2 1

*This book is dedicated to all the amazing women and men
whom we have worked with in our workshops and retreats,
in recognition of their courage to take their journey
—and do whatever it takes—
to wake up and manifest their higher potential.*

Table of Contents

Foreword

In this lovely and practical introduction to the Enneagram, Beatrice Chestnut, PhD and Uranio Paes explore the nine core personality patterns and how they shape and inform our lives. These patterns are the source of many important mental, emotional, and behavioral habits, which affect who we believe ourselves to be and how we engage with life. By grasping the full significance of those patterns, you can achieve a higher level of self-awareness and the emotional freedom that comes from seeing and breaking free from unconscious defenses.

Each chapter will help you see those defenses in action, and each provides a step-by-step guide to "waking up." By "waking up" we mean lessening the constraints of self-limiting "habits" that motivate feelings, thoughts, and behaviors. We all have such habits. They can be very hard to "see" because they have become so familiar and comfortable over the course of your life. Why? Because they are deeply embedded in the ways our minds have learned to make sense of the world and our relationships with others. *The Enneagram Guide for Waking Up* provides valuable tools for bringing these patterns to awareness. In the process, you can develop a fresh understanding of your personal story, including the joys and traumas of your childhood, and how that story informs how you function as an adult.

Like Chestnut and Paes, we also view individual personality differences as a combination of nature and nurture—our innate inheritance and the ways in which our unique life experience shapes us. And our Enneagram study also began with the pioneering work of David Daniels, MD, and Helen Palmer, and their Narrative Enneagram school. In our own work, we examine these personality patterns in the context of interpersonal neurobiology. We consider how they may emerge through systems of mind that enable us to operate in the world as we seek safety and certainty, connections with others, and a sense of agency and power in our lives. We share the view that a deeper understanding of these patterns can lead us to grow into better human beings. This, after all, is the original purpose of the Enneagram.

Many people who encounter the Enneagram seek clear guidance on "what to do" to further their growth once they identify their core Enneagram pattern. This book offers answers, grounded in Bea's and Uranio's many years of working with the Enneagram as teachers and practitioners. We appreciate the way this book builds on the solid foundation of the teaching of David Daniels and Helen Palmer to clarify how each type of person can apply the information provided by this remarkable tool to grow beyond the level of ego, or personality, at which we get stuck moving through life on "autopilot."

To make the most of the valuable information offered in this book, we urge you to approach it with curiosity, as well as commitment! Our minds are fascinating. Changing them involves work, to be sure, but don't neglect the opportunity to enjoy the journey of growing and expanding through this exciting approach to self-discovery. The mindful strategies and wise advice contained in this approachable guide will help you create more freedom and richer relationships in your life, and more peace in our world!

—DANIEL J. SIEGEL, MD,
author of *The Developing Mind* and *Parenting From the Inside Out*,
and THE PATTERNS OF DEVELOPMENTAL PATHWAYS GROUP

• • •

The Patterns of Developmental Pathways Group is a team of five medical and social scientists—Daniel J. Siegel MD, Laura Baker PhD, David Daniels, MD (1934–2017), Denise Daniels PhD, and Jack Killen MD—who have been exploring the Enneagram's personality patterns from the perspective of contemporary science for over ten years. A book describing their work is forthcoming.

Introduction

The only person you are destined to become is the person you decide to be.

RALPH WALDO EMERSON

You are not your personality. But who are you?

If you're like most people, you picked up this book because you want to understand more about why you are the way you are. Why do you do the things you do or react the way you do to certain things? Why, no matter how many times you think you've learned something, do you keep making the same mistakes? How you can make your relationships better and what happened in the one that didn't work out? Why is there one issue in your life that you just can't get past?

Well, there's a reason for all of these things. And there's a reason why you have a difficult time understanding why you do what you do.

Basically—you have become a zombie.

No, we're not saying you're literally one of the undead. We're saying you're going through life in a zombie-like state—on autopilot, "asleep" to who you really are and what's really going on inside you. Just like most of us do.

This book can help awaken you from this state by introducing you to the Enneagram, a powerful growth tool based on timeless wisdom that can help you come to know your true self. The Enneagram can free you from defensive self-limiting patterns and help you grow into an expanded version of yourself. It can show you who you really are by showing you who you *think* you are. Only then can you know who you *actually* are—and who you are not.

What Is the Enneagram?

The Enneagram is a complex and meaningful symbol that relates to many different systems of knowledge, including psychology, cosmology, and mathematics. It forms the basis of a highly accurate typology that describes nine distinct personality types and serves as a sense-making framework for understanding the human ego and mapping out a process of growth. As a psychological and spiritual model that lays out specific paths of self-development, it helps us "wake up" to ourselves by revealing the habitual patterns and blind spots that limit our growth and transformation.

The Enneagram is based on nine personality types grounded in three "centers of intelligence" that determine how we take in and process information from the outside world.

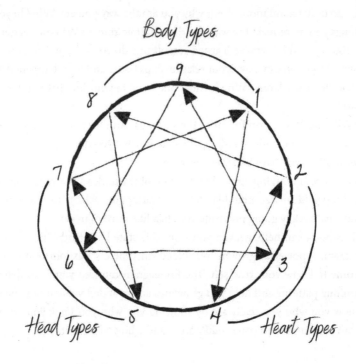

- We think and analyze using our head center. Types 5, 6, and 7 are dominated by this center and their experience is shaped by thoughts. They are analytical and imaginative, and know how to plan and make sense of things, but they can be overly logical and detached from feelings and emotions.

- We feel emotions and connect with others using our heart center. Types 2, 3, and 4 are dominated by this center and their experience is shaped by feelings. They are usually emotionally intelligent and empathetic, and value connection and relationships, but they can be overly focused on image and fear rejection.

- We experience life through our senses using our body center. Types 1, 8, and 9 are dominated by this center and their experience is shaped by sensations. They are usually committed and responsible, and value truth and honor, but they can be judgmental and inflexible.

We get "out of balance" when we use one of these centers more than the other two. The Enneagram helps us become aware of and redress this imbalance.

Each of the nine types on the Enneagram circle can be defined in terms of a central survival strategy comprised of habitual patterns and motivations. We all develop unconscious strategies to avoid pain and discomfort as we move through the world. When we see ourselves as the sum total of these unconscious patterns, we lose sight of who we really are and what's possible for us. The fact that these strategies are unconscious makes it hard (or impossible) to acknowledge and move beyond them. But we are actually much more than we think we are, and the Enneagram helps us to realize this.

Each of the nine personality types on the Enneagram circle has three distinct "subtypes," making for a total of twenty-seven types. These subtypes are more nuanced versions of the original nine types and are defined by three instinctual drives: self-preservation, social belonging, and sexual (one-to-one) fusion. Each subtype reveals how these instinctual drives shape behavior and express our core emotional motivations. For each type, the three subtype personalities take slightly different shapes, including one of the three, called a "counter-type," that goes against the general expression of the type in some ways, because the emotional driver and the instinctual goal go in opposite directions.

To unlock the amazing insights of the Enneagram, you must first identify which of the nine types best matches your personality, then identify the subtype that most accurately describes you. This can be a challenging task, however, because different types look similar on the surface and you may identify with more than one. The fact that the type descriptions refer in part to *unconscious* habits, or blind spots, makes the task all the more challenging

At one level, these personality types are based on a very simple thing— where we focus our attention as we move through the world. But what we see also defines what we *don't* see—as well as the fact that we don't see it. These are our blind spots. When we remain unaware of these key aspects of our experience, we stay blind to the impact they have on how we think, feel, and act. And this explains why we can be said to be "asleep"—going through life like zombies.

To "wake up" from this state, we must confront the ego—as well as the Shadow cast by the ego. We need to become aware of the automatic habits that structure our defensive egoic persona, as well as all that remains unconscious in us connected to our ego's need to protect itself. This self-protective persona keeps us focused on *its* needs and prevents us from feeling pain—or joy—condemning us to a kind of waking sleep in which we don't know who we are and what's possible for us. We suppress these Shadow elements because they create pain or challenge our self-image. By making these elements more conscious, however, we become more self-aware and whole. Without facing them, we can never know ourselves as we actually are. When we don't see and own the unconscious tendencies connected to the personality we stay focused on (and limited by), we are held hostage to who we think we are, or who we fear we are, or who we would like to be. When we move beyond the ego and actively engage in the process of growth that the Enneagram maps out for us, we begin to awaken to our full potential.

Making and Waking a Zombie

Over time, we learn to equate all of who we are with the ego, creating a kind of false self or persona. We each come into this world as a unique and authentic self. As dependent children, however, we adopt survival strategies to help us adapt to our environment. We find ingenious ways to navigate through life using coping strategies to protect ourselves as small beings in a big world. These unconscious strategies determine to which of the nine personality types we belong.

But "you" and "your personality" are *not* the same thing. Our personalities help us survive childhood, but limit our conscious awareness of all we can be in adulthood. Slowly, over time, our need to survive in the world causes us to develop false selves that stand in place of our true selves. And the farther we get from childhood, the more our true selves are obscured by the defensive patterns we adopt. We become trapped in these invisible, habitual patterns and it becomes difficult to grow beyond them as they become more deeply ingrained. They become fixed and rigid in ways we don't recognize, precisely because they help us adapt and survive—in some cases, under difficult conditions. As we become more comfortable with these strategies, we descend deeper and deeper into a zombie state without even knowing it.

The Enneagram helps us understand how the survival strategies we develop early in life can turn us into zombies later in life. It gives us techniques for consciously and intentionally awakening so we can come to know our true selves. When we "fall asleep" to our true selves and our enormous potential, we lose sight of our innate capacity for growth beyond the ego. We get stuck at a low level of consciousness and forget that we can choose a higher state of awareness.

Awakening to our true selves and moving toward this greater consciousness requires an enormous amount of intentional effort. We must become *aware* of our zombie-like state and then actively work against it in order to rise above it. We must engage in intentional, conscious inner work to awaken from the trance we enter when we think we *are* our personality. We must continually remind ourselves to be more present and attuned to our moment-to-moment experience to overcome the deeply rooted habits of the ego. Without this conscious effort, we can remain zombies all our lives. And many people do. The Enneagram can help us understand the patterns and tendencies that may be blocking our own awakening.

How to Use This Book

Each chapter in this book describes a distinct path of transformation for one of the nine personality types. Each traces an individualized journey—from realizing problematic egoic patterns, to specific steps in the process of self-discovery, to experiencing more freedom from self-limiting constraints. You needn't read this book from cover to cover; you can skip straight to the chapter you think best describes your personality type.

Finding your type can be a valuable learning process in itself. First, try to discover your type using the checklists given at the beginning of each chapter and reflect on which type fits best with what you know about yourself. Confirm what you find through a deep exploration of what feels most true for you. Get input from people in your life whom you trust to help you see your blind spots. Try not to distract yourself from your development journey, however, by becoming too focused on diagnosis and description. No one piece of data will give you the final answer; you have to put all the pieces together.

Once you find your type, it may show you aspects of your personality that you don't want to acknowledge. Have the courage to own these traits. Some people see the Enneagram as negative. Understandably, they feel implicitly judged by it. But you aren't being judged. And you must not judge yourself. Cultivate self-compassion. The Enneagram is about understanding the truth—and the truth can hurt. It's hard work to wake up and it's natural to avoid feeling pain. But you must feel your pain in order to awaken.

Each chapter begins with an allegory that introduces the key themes of the type. We then describe a three-stage path to transformation, as well as the blind spots and pain points you may encounter along the way. To make progress on this growth journey, we provide specific suggestions for how you can leverage the insights you gain about your type to further your growth. The transformational power of the Enneagram comes in part from what are called "wings"—the two personality types that are adjacent to your type on the Enneagram circle—and "arrows"—the lines that connect you to two other personality types on the circle. The wing points suggest gentle developmental steps you can take, while the arrow lines indicate more radical developmental shifts you can achieve through conscious intention. After you learn to become more aware of the unconscious tendencies of your main type, you can create further conscious growth shifts beyond your type's fixed perspective by integrating the healthy qualities of these of adjacent and opposing types to embody more of your true self and move forward on your path.

Each chapter also describes a "paradox" that is grounded in the polarity between the passion that acts as the core emotional driver of the type, and the virtue that represents its higher-level awareness. Each type's passion reflects a kind of zombie addiction to seeing the world through the lens of this core emotional driver. Each virtue represents the goal toward which the type travels on its path of transformation. You move forward on your path by integrating your Shadow—the darker aspects of your type and the habitual patterns and blind spots that characterize it. The original meaning of the word "passion" is "to suffer." Thus your awakening comes in large part from the "conscious suffering" you endure as you face your Shadow.

The Enneagram addresses the challenges we face as we try to awaken to our "high side." It maps out the ways in which we function and gives us tools to become consciously aware of the ways in which we sleep-walk through life. We all become zombies by forgetting who we really are, but each of us becomes trapped in a specific set of unconscious habits. The chapters that follow highlight the ways in which each of us can take our own unique journey of awakening and learn to rediscover our true selves.

Embark on your journey and enjoy the adventure!

The
Enneagram
Guide to Waking Up

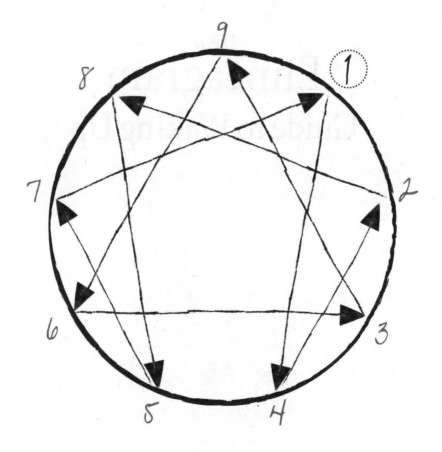

The Path from Anger to Serenity

Your best teacher is your last mistake.

RALPH NADER

O nce upon a time, there was a person named One. He came into this world as a spontaneous child ready to appreciate the inherent perfection of life. Completely serene and accepting, he felt free to experience joy and fun in everything he did. He took things lightly and flowed flexibly with life, with himself, and with everyone around him.

But early in life, One had a painful experience of feeling criticized. When this happened, he felt pressured to conform to others' standards of good behavior. One unconsciously tried to cope with the pain of feeling judged and punished by proactively monitoring and criticizing himself before others had a chance to. He internalized the standards others applied to him and tried to be good and do the right thing all the time. He began to feel that he had to be perfect to be seen as worthy, and that he had to work hard to control himself in order to be "good."

In his quest to be good, One developed an ability to notice and correct his own errors, to see how everything he did could be more perfect, and to determine what needed to be improved in the world around him. He worked hard to uphold the highest standards of good behavior and he judged people harshly who didn't follow the rules. He became excellent at making things excellent—including himself. He evaluated everything he saw in terms of how bad or wrong it was—most of all himself.

Over time, One became very good at being virtuous and avoiding mistakes. He found the best ways to do things and adhered to all the rules of good behavior all the time. He criticized himself whenever something turned out imperfectly (which was all the time) and he tried to do better the next time. But in the process of getting better and being better, One lost touch with many aspects of himself. He stopped feeling or doing anything that might have even the smallest chance of being considered wrong. He lost most of his awareness of his instinctual impulses, his feelings, his creativity, and his spontaneity. He lost touch with his own inner sense of what felt right, but might be judged as wrong.

By imposing strict limits on himself, One learned to avoid anything that could possibly be wrong, including his own deepest rhythms, wishes, and dreams. He often became very angry when others didn't follow the rules, but, instead of expressing his anger, he hid his feelings and tried to be nice. He prioritized being ethical, reliable, and responsible in everything he did. He felt compelled to control everything he possibly could to make sure that he got things right every time. And he punished himself when he didn't. His survival strategy wouldn't let him do anything else. And he felt irritated about *that* too—but couldn't let anyone know that he felt irritated.

What One didn't realize was that everyone around him *did* know he was angry because, when he enforced what was right, he often stomped around or banged his fists on the table or talked in a sarcastic tone of voice. It became part of the way he operated when in survival mode. He didn't necessarily like it—in fact, it was very hard on him—but he couldn't stop it. He couldn't acknowledge his anger, because being angry was not good. Sometimes he felt tired and sad as a result—almost letting himself feel. But what could he do?

One eventually became completely deadened to any real sense of himself. He "fell asleep" to his own inherent goodness—a goodness that revealed itself in his good intentions and his genuine desire to be a good person. He could only keep following the rules and working hard to meet the highest standards in everything he did. But he also completely lost awareness of his deeper human need for fun and relaxation, as well as his basic human wish to be bad once in a while.

One had become a zombie—a very polite, appropriate, rule-following zombie, but a zombie just the same.

THE TYPE 1 CHECKLIST

If most or all of the following personality traits apply to you, you may be a Type 1 personality:

- ☑ You have a harsh inner critic that monitors what you do and operates most of the time; you are sensitive to criticism from others.

- ☑ You naturally sort perceptions into "good or bad," "right or wrong"; you try hard to be good and do the right thing.

- ☑ When you look at almost anything, you automatically see how it could be improved; you easily notice errors and want to correct them.

- ☑ You follow the rules all or most of the time; you think the world would be better off if everyone did the same.

- ☑ You think and talk in terms of "shoulds" and "musts"; most or all of the time, you believe duty has to come before pleasure.

- ☑ You place a high value on being a good, responsible, and reliable person; you have high standards for yourself and others; you are an advocate for self-improvement.

- ☑ You over-control your emotions because you believe it's inappropriate or unproductive to express them or act on them.

- ☑ You over-control your impulses for fun and pleasure.

- ☑ You believe there is one right way to do everything, which happens to be your way; you have strong opinions and readily express them.

☑ You value the rare occasions on which something you do or see feels absolutely perfect; this inspires you to keep striving to make things as good as they can possibly be.

If, after using the Type 1 checklist, you find that you are Type 1, your growth journey will follow three steps.

First, you will embark on a quest to know yourself by learning to identify personality patterns connected to the need to be right, do the right thing, and improve yourself and the world around you.

Next, you must face your Shadow to become more aware of unconscious patterns and tendencies that stem from your need to feel worthy and virtuous to quell a basic sense of anxiety or prove your inherent goodness. This helps you to recognize all the ways criticism and self-criticism are actually holding you back.

The final stage of your journey involves moving toward the "high side" of your type by relaxing your need to be good and accepting your natural human impulses. When you do this, you begin to recognize the inherent goodness in yourself and others, and appreciate imperfection as part of the organic flow of life.

> "People will do anything, no matter how absurd, in order to avoid facing their own soul." —C. G. Jung

EMBARKING ON THE QUEST

If you are a Type 1, the first stage of your path of awakening involves learning to observe yourself more consciously. This means developing the ability to notice your specific habits of judging yourself and others—without judging yourself further for judging. Your growth journey will involve acknowledging how much attention you pay to correcting errors in your environment, monitoring and criticizing the things you do, and resenting what others are doing that isn't right. To further your journey, you will need to work to feel less responsible (or overly responsible) for making sure things happen the right way, begin to respect your emotions and impulses, and develop a greater capacity for compassion for yourself. By learning to recognize when you are overly focused on self-improvement—how you try to be good and avoid being bad—you advance down the path toward greater self-knowledge.

Key Type 1 Patterns

To embark on your journey, focus on and make more conscious these five habitual Type 1 patterns.

Criticizing Yourself

Notice if you have an "inner critic"—an internal voice or sense through which you continually monitor yourself and others. That voice provides critical commentary about what's happening, judging everything as "good" or "bad." You may tend to be unaware of the consequences of this self-monitoring, especially when your inner critic is harsh—which it will be. You likely ignore the physical, emotional, and mental tension this critic causes when it enforces what it defines as good behavior at the high cost of increased stress.

Requiring Perfection

You put pressure on yourself to meet very high standards and this can lead to tension or procrastination when nothing ever seems good enough. Your focus on imperfection generates a negative attitude about life and may cause you to make people feel criticized or judged. You probably find it hard to relax, enjoy what's happening, and celebrate successes when your judging mind continually dwells on how the results you achieve could be better or more perfect. When you recognize this, you can begin to refocus these thoughts and move toward a more positive attitude.

Following the Rules

Observe yourself to see if you rigidly adhere to rules, routines, structures, and processes, and you create rules for others as well. You may become angry when people don't follow the rules in the ways you think they should or adhere to your standards of correct behavior, though you likely avoid fully acknowledging your anger. You may rather experience this anger as resentment toward people who do "bad" things you would never allow yourself to do. Why are they free to do whatever they want when you can't? Notice if you tend to display a similar rigidity concerning ethics, morals, and work.

Sacrificing Pleasure

You probably work too hard and find it difficult to make time to relax. Does work always have to come before play for you? Observe yourself to see if it feels challenging to try to stop controlling everything and just flow with the rhythm of life. You have likely forgotten or ignore the early experiences that made you feel as if you had to suppress your desires. Notice if you conform to a set of unquestioned rules, but don't fully realize how stressful it feels to hold yourself to such high standards. You hesitate to pursue pleasure or allow for leisure time to just enjoy yourself.

Controlling Emotions

When you do somehow allow yourself to express feelings and instinctual reactions, you likely do so with a lot of self-criticism and self-blame. When you avoid being aware of anger, notice if that anger leaks out as partially repressed feelings like irritation, frustration, annoyance, self-righteousness, or body tension. When you find yourself judging emotions as unproductive or inappropriate, see if you tend to rationalize your tendency to suppress them, citing good reasons to over-control your feelings. Notice if you judge yourself and others as "bad" for expressing anger and other emotions as a way to enforce your habitual avoidance of your feelings.

> "At the core of all anger is a need that is not being fulfilled."
> —Marshall Rosenberg

The Type 1 Passion

Anger is the passion that drives Type 1s. It often manifests as a preoccupation with self-judgment and striving to be good. As the core emotional motivation of this type, anger usually appears in a contained or partially contained form. Type 1s often don't express it directly, because they feel motivated to suppress it and direct it mostly at themselves. They avoid communicating anger because they prioritize the need to be "good," and believe that anger makes them "bad." This anger can thus be understood as a state of upset or displeasure that people or things are not as they should be.

Type 1s usually don't experience themselves as "angry" in an obvious way, however. Their survival strategies focus on goodness, virtue, and correctness, so they tend to control their underlying anger—to the point of not even seeing themselves as angry. In their drive to be "good" and express what is "appropriate" according to conventional social norms, they try *not* to be aware of their anger, sometimes over-controlling it without realizing how angry they really feel.

When we suppress our naturally occurring emotions, however, they don't go away. So when Type 1s unconsciously avoid feeling their anger, it nonetheless leaks out in repressed forms like criticism, annoyance, irritation, frustration, or self-righteousness, reflecting an intolerance of how things are. It creates an emotional atmosphere of dissatisfaction and unease when they can't change things to be more just, more perfect, or ideal. It may also leak out in physical ways—as tension held in the body or a particular tone of voice.

If you identify with this type, here are some typical manifestations of your anger that you must observe and make conscious to move forward on your path to awakening:

- Determined and watchful overseeing of what's happening.

- Self-criticism and criticism or judgment of others.

- Efforts at improvement or self-improvement, as well as attempts to regulate, control, or correct what's happening to make it conform to an ideal or high standard of quality.

- Direct or indirect expression of annoyance, irritation, or frustration.

- Passive-aggressive behaviors.

- Self-righteousness; advocating or fighting for social justice or political reform; efforts to "do the right thing" or set things right.

- Shame, guilt, or self-blame—activities of the super-ego.

- Body tension and physical rigidity.

- Sarcasm and mocking or critical tone of voice.

"Being honest may not get you a lot of friends but it'll always get you the right ones." —John Lennon

Using Type 1 Wings as Growth Stretches

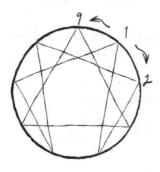

The two types adjacent to Type 1 on the Enneagram circle are Types 2 and 9. By reaching toward the healthy qualities of Type 9, Type 1s can become more adaptable and learn to relax. By integrating the positive traits of Type 2, they become more adept at relationships. This moves them beyond their usual focus on maintaining high standards and working to achieve an ideal of perfection, and helps them understand their habit of characterizing things in terms of "right and wrong," and "good and bad."

- First, adopt Type 9's ability to go with the flow, adapt to the agenda of others, and relax and just be. Develop an ability to create harmony in your environment by noticing points of agreement (rather than difference) with the people around you. Find common ground when interacting with others and expand your usual viewpoint from what could be improved to what already works well. Spend more time listening to others' opinions and less time asserting your own. Consciously work against your tendency to judge by appreciating and supporting what's going on around you without finding fault with it. Prioritize others' "right ways" of seeing or doing over your own and allow yourself to enjoy connecting with those around you.

- Then integrate Type 2's ability to focus less on tasks and processes, and more on people and relationships. Develop an increased capacity to create rapport with others by expressing interest in them, tuning in to how they feel, or sharing your emotions. Communicate with people according to how they feel or what they want and be more flexible and diplomatic when collaborating with others. Balance your tendency to evaluate and judge with an ability to sense what others need and find ways to provide them with resources or support. Make it an intentional practice to see the best in others instead of noticing errors that need to be corrected.

. . . .
"The simple act of caring is heroic." —Edward Albert
. . . .

FACING THE SHADOW

The second stage of the Type 1 growth journey is all about acknowledging and owning your tendency to punish yourself and repress your emotions and instinctual impulses. This helps you realize that your focus on doing things right and improving everything can actually be a bad habit.

A big challenge for this type lies in the fact that they try to repress parts of themselves that they believe make them bad or unworthy. They try to be "good," but this usually means eliminating any awareness of anything they might judge as "bad," including mistakes, uncontained emotional outbursts, normal instinctual impulses, and important human feelings. This lack of self-awareness can make them critical, rigid, and intolerant, even while they consciously think they are being righteous, moral, and virtuous. Ironically, they must learn not to improve, but rather to "get worse" by accepting the risk (or the reality) of being "bad" or "wrong"—starting with small things. They make progress on their growth journey only when they become less serious and less concerned about doing everything perfectly.

Meeting the Type 1 Shadow

If you identify as a Type 1, here are some actions you can take to become more aware of and counteract key Type 1 unconscious patterns, blind spots, and pain points:

- Lessen your focus on listening to your inner critic and find ways to stop judging yourself and others. Criticism creates more problems than it solves. It adds to your stress and alienates people.

- Become conscious of the anger underlying your irritability. What is it about? How do you suppress it? How does it leak out when you don't allow yourself to feel it? Embrace anger and learn to see it as positive.

- Learn to express emotions and impulses actively, and notice when you have feelings you don't communicate. Become aware of any impulses you resist and ask yourself why.

- Be less responsible. Take on fewer duties as urgent priorities and reduce your tendency to micromanage and be excessively detail-oriented.

- Be more flexible and open to innovation and change. Plan activities that force you to become more spontaneous and less tense.

- Break the rules—not just the ones you judge as bad rules.

- Don't judge yourself for making mistakes or worry excessively about the consequences. Work on forgiving yourself more.

- Engage in activities that allow you to have moments of relaxation and fun. Act on impulses for pleasure and focus more on fun than control.

- Let yourself be bad. Forget about self-improvement and doing the right thing for a while.

"There is no light without shadow, and no psychic wholeness without imperfection." —C. G. Jung

The Type 1 Blind Spots

This type holds on to the illusion that perfection is possible, achievable, and desirable—and then they criticize themselves for all the inevitable ways they fall short and fail to get it right when trying to meet these impossible standards. Their blind spots tend to hide all the human stuff they don't want to see while they try so hard to do things perfectly. They deny and bury all the messy truths connected to being a normal person in an imperfect world.

Type 1 blind spots may include emotions (both "good" and "bad"), deep desires to do what they really want to do—and possibly even a secret wish to be bad. They face the challenge of owning and embracing all the parts of themselves they have demonized to justify maintaining control. They may resist acknowledging these blind spots because their default mode is so much about "doing the right thing" and being a good person. They may fear that chaos and disorder will be unleashed if they accept what they judge as "bad" in themselves.

If you identify as a Type 1, here are some unconscious habitual patterns you must bring to the surface, confront, and work to make more conscious to move forward on your journey.

Avoiding Anger

Do you avoid feeling or expressing your anger? Does your unacknowledged anger sometimes leak out in repressed forms like irritation, tension, stiffness, frustration, annoyance, and self-righteousness? Try some of these techniques to integrate this blind spot:

- Pay attention to signs of anger (or suppressed versions of anger) and allow yourself to feel it.

- Analyze any fears you may have about being angry and make them conscious. Cultivate more conscious awareness of how angry you are.

- Acknowledge any judgments you make about being angry or expressing anger. Notice and question any beliefs you have about the "inappropriateness" of feeling angry.

- Consider how your anger can be channeled in positive ways when made conscious—fighting injustice, establishing boundaries, promoting practices that support good causes, or calling out behavior that hurts people.

- Recognize and learn to embrace other emotions like sadness, pain, enthusiasm, and joy. When you repress one emotion, you usually push others out of your consciousness as well.

Criticizing Yourself and Others

Do you often catch yourself in the act of criticizing yourself? Do you justify being harsh on yourself based on the idea that self-criticism is necessary to enforce good behavior? Do you frequently criticize others? What happens in your relationships when others feel criticized by you? Here are some actions you can take to integrate this blind spot:

- Observe yourself closely when your inner critic gets going. What does this feel like? Does it increase your stress level? Allow yourself to feel the hurt you may be inflicting on yourself. Notice when you "normalize" what amounts to self-punishment.

- Be more aware of how you enforce your high standards. What beliefs lie behind your tendency to impose these standards on yourself and others?

- Ask someone you know and trust if they have ever felt criticized by you. Ask them how that made them feel.

- Inquire into the motives of your "inner critic." What assumptions do you make that drive your tendency to be self-critical? What do you fear will happen if you don't criticize yourself?

- Contemplate whether what you criticize in others is something that you have an unconscious desire to do.

- Notice how often you tell someone that they are doing something wrong. How do you talk to yourself if you think you have done something wrong?

Neglecting Relaxation

How often do you allow yourself to rest and relax? What taboos do you have (and regularly enforce) about prioritizing pleasure above duty? How often do you do what you are supposed to do rather than what you would like to do? Here are some actions you can take to integrate this blind spot:

- Do something you judge as "bad." Break the rules; put off work to go have fun; intentionally do something the wrong way. How does this feel?

- Tune in to your body and really notice how tense you are.

- For a whole day, inject humor and lightness into everything you say and do. Notice what happens.

- Notice your tendency to over-control yourself. Observe how you hold back impulses and emotions. What happens as a result? How much energy does this take?

- Experiment with irresponsibility. What kinds of things do you do every day that you think you *must* do that you really don't have to do?

- Spend a whole day having fun and relaxing (when you have things to do). Don't do anything you "should" do. How hard is this? How does it feel?

> "We don't forgive for others, we forgive for ourselves."
> —Desmond Tutu

Type 1 Pain

To experience the pain they have avoided by building and identifying with the defensive habits that make up their personality, Type 1s must consciously feel the emotions of their inner child who felt hurt when criticized early on. They must feel *all* their anger and all of what's beneath it—any pain or hurt or sadness that came from being punished or pushed to conform to external demands.

This type may repress happiness along with other emotions, perhaps fearing that the experience of joy may lead to a dangerous preference for feeling happy over doing things right. They may believe that freedom will lead to disorder and mayhem. But when they acknowledge all their emotions and see them as important and valid, they no longer need to deny the truth of what they feel to uphold impossible standards. This constitutes an important part of their liberation.

If you identify with Type 1, it can be difficult to acknowledge specific feelings you avoid because you believe them to be inappropriate, wrong, or dangerous. But you must allow yourself to accept these feelings in order to grow. You will ultimately feel better if you can learn to tolerate this specific pain to achieve a fuller realization of your real self. Remember, only zombies feel no pain. Here are some steps you can take to acknowledge and deal with your pain:

- Become aware of the anger you feel and why you feel it. Explore all the anger "derivatives" like irritation, frustration, impatience, body tension, and self-righteousness. The more you can experience and study your anger in all its forms, the more free you will eventually feel. Consider the good reasons you have for being angry.

- Analyze the fear that makes you believe bad things will happen if you allow yourself to ackowledge how angry you really are.

- Consider how hard you have been on yourself for so long, and feel grief for the child who had to suppress its own natural impulses and instincts to minimize criticism and punishment.

- Acknowledge the pain behind all your efforts at self-control through self-criticism—the pain of being punished for being "bad" when you probably weren't really doing anything wrong. Confront the anxiety you feel about making mistakes and the guilt that accompanies your need to control yourself.

- Explore any feelings of shame and embarrassment you experience when you indulge your natural impulses.

- Identify any feelings of happiness or joy that you pushed aside because of your need to control yourself.

"Where there is anger, there is always pain underneath."
—Eckhart Tolle

The Type 1 Subtypes

Identifying your Type 1 subtype can help you more precisely target your efforts to confront your blind spots, unconscious tendencies, and hidden pain. The specific patterns and tendencies of the subtypes vary depending on which of the three survival instincts dominates your experience.

Self-Preservation 1 Subtype

This subtype experiences the most worry and anxiety and pursues perfection the most aggressively. They usually feel they have to be overly responsible from an early age, and so have a fear about survival. They are the most self-critical and least critical of others. They repress anger the most, and so don't relate to being angry. Their anger leaks out as body tension, micromanagement, or resentment—or the need to control everything. They are, however, the warmest and friendliest subtype.

Social 1 Subtype

This subtype is less perfectionist and more "perfect"—at least from the outside. They focus on finding the right or best way to do things, then teach it to others. They tend to be the most intellectual subtype and may appear superior because they channel their anger into being "the owners of truth." They are partly successful at repressing anger, so tend to appear "cool" and not as anxious. They focus on injustice or working for social causes, but they don't feel comfortable in the middle of a group. They often assume the role of leader to model their own rectitude for others.

Sexual (One-to-One) 1 Subtype

This is the only Type 1 subtype that feels more comfortable with anger. They tend to express anger more than the other subtypes, even though they also sometimes control it. They are more critical of others than they are of themselves, although they are still self-critical. They claim connection to a higher moral authority and are more often reformers than perfectionists. They are zealous when advocating for what they see as right, for what needs to be fixed, and for their right to get what they want.

. . . .
"Worry often gives a small thing a big shadow."
—Swedish Proverb
. . . .

The Type 1 Subtype Shadows

You can more effectively confront your own Shadow if you know the specific shadow characteristics of your Type 1 subtype. Below are some of the shadow aspects of each subtype. Because the behavior typical of each subtype can be highly automatic, these traits can be hardest to see and own.

Self-Preservation 1 Shadow

If this is your subtype, you maintain a high level of anxiety and worry about everything you do. But you never really feel that things turn out right enough, so you never really feel okay. You unconsciously repress anger to the point where you express its opposite—you appear very polite and friendly. You internalize the anger you repress so that it fuels self-criticism and becomes trapped in your body. You feel the need to control every detail of everything you do.

You fret about making everything perfect all the time—including yourself. To grow, you will need to find ways to ease your anxiety and become more aware of your anger.

Social 1 Shadow

If this is your subtype, you put a great deal of effort into finding the right—or perfect—way to do something, then become rigid about conforming to that right way. You partially repress anger, so that it fuels an unconscious need to be intellectually or morally superior in the things you do. You need to be the perfect role model to teach others the right way to do things, but you don't see how this sets you above and apart from others. You assert your own rectitude as an outlet for repressed anger and the need for power and control. It will be good for you to work to become more flexible and less perfect.

Sexual (One-to-One) 1 Shadow

If this is your subtype, you express a need to perfect others and reform society so that whatever happens conforms to your sense of what is right, perfect, or just. You criticize others as a way to assert your moral authority. You vent anger and unconsciously avoid taking responsibility for correcting your own flawed perspective or actions. You have a strong need to control what's happening. Your need to get what you want confirms your sense of what's right and you avoid questioning your own standards or authority. You rationalize your right to take what you need or fix what needs to be fixed when anger fuels desire.

. . . .

"Happiness can exist only in acceptance."
—George Orwell

. . . .

The Type 1 Paradox

The Type 1 paradox is grounded in the polarity between the passion of anger and the virtue of serenity. For this type, recognizing the compulsion they have to be right and call attention to what's not right—their need to go against what is happening to make things more perfect—helps them understand how the passion of anger operates. They move toward a state of serenity by becoming more aware of how anger drives them. Serenity can be understood as a state of being totally peaceful within, while fully accepting the way people and things are. When they aim at being more serene and peaceful, they start to let go of their need to be right and their drive to be perfect. They become capable of surrendering to the fact that things may often seem imperfect, but they can be perfect in their imperfection.

If you identify as a Type 1, here are some steps you can take toward becoming more conscious of your anger and more open to a higher state of serenity:

- Notice when you feel tension in your body related to a desire to correct or adjust what happens in the world around you.

- Observe all the ways you habitually resist relaxation and avoid lowering both your inner standards and your external vigilance. Let go of your need to alter or change anything—inside or outside yourself.

- Pay attention to any physical tension you feel and consciously try to let it go. Relax whatever tension you are holding and notice how this makes you feel—both emotionally and physically.

- Admit when you feel angry and investigate the sources and consequences of your anger. Be aware of both your anger and any sense you have of needing to hold it back or control it. What would happen if you just accepted your anger and embraced it as a sign of how much you care?

- Work on having compassion for yourself—both for the inherent imperfection of your personality and for the inner conflict you experience in trying to demonstrate excellence in all you do. Ask yourself whether you would rather be right or happy.

- Consider that perhaps everything is "okay" just as it is, that you don't have to intervene to improve anything. Ask yourself how important your objections to reality really are. Focus on acceptance.

. . . .
"Peace is not a relationship of nations. It is a condition of mind brought about by a serenity of soul." —Jawaharlal Nehru
. . . .

Using Type 1 Arrow Lines for Growth

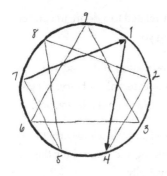

The two types connected to Type 1 by the internal arrow lines within the Enneagram diagram are Types 4 and 7. By integrating Type 4's ability to access emotions, this type makes a big shift in balancing out their usual focus on getting things right and avoiding blame; by developing Type 7's tendency to explore possibilities and think more creatively, they can become more relaxed and more able to innovate.

- First, embody the healthy qualities of Type 7 by allowing yourself to explore possibilities and think more creatively instead of adhering to your usual routines and rules. Brainstorm ideas about innovative ways to do things. See the value in more flexible ways of thinking and acting. Instead of looking for errors to correct, look for opportunities to be hedonistic and self-indulgent. Prioritize pleasure and playfulness in your life and integrate more lightness, humor, and sociability into your world. Quit work early to go have fun. Relax your high standards and let yourself do things in playful or exciting ways rather than the "right" ways.

- Then integrate the healthy qualities of Type 4 by consciously getting more in touch with deeper emotions. What makes you truly happy? What makes you feel sad? Explore any pain, grief, or anger you have been pushing away, knowing that any kind of experience of authentic emotion can feel good after repressing your feelings for so long. Intentionally do things to express yourself creatively rather than following your habitual processes and routines. Do what you want to do, not just what your inner critic says you "should" do. Ask yourself what has meaning for you and let that guide you. Act from a sense of purpose rather than a sense of duty or responsibility.

. . . .
"You can't stop the waves, but you can learn to surf."
—Joseph Goldstein
. . . .

EMBRACING THE HIGH SIDE

On the third part of their journey, Type 1s accept that they don't need to work so hard or be perfect to be loved. They embrace the idea that they are worthy and good enough just by being themselves. They become more content with who they are by accepting—and even appreciating—imperfection, and seeing that everything in the world is perfectly imperfect.

When this type learns to trust their own worth, they trust that whatever happens comes about as part of a larger flow they don't need to manage, direct, oppose, or improve. When they don't have to prove their worth by doing every-thing right, they realize they have the power to choose to be more free. And this realization can liberate them from the constant effort to prove their worth. They can then live more from their own natural rhythms and preferences. They can do what makes them happy, rather than what makes them right. They can embody more humor and lightness in everything they do. When they achieve this higher state, they become a joy to be around.

If you identify with this type, you relax into a sense of calm and peace when you begin to manifest more of your higher side, knowing intuitively that you have done the inner work necessary to transcend your ego's conviction that everything needs to be perfected. As this sense of peace grows, you become more and more able to rise above your judging mindset. Here are some things you can do on this part of your journey that you couldn't have done before:

- Learn to feel deeply relaxed—both physically and emotionally. When you feel relaxed, you can let some of the instinctual impulses you have been holding back come into your life and channel them wisely. You can appreciate and benefit from the inherent wisdom of your body and your instincts.

- Accept and feel a sense of peace with yourself and others. Understand that we are all inherently good, "right," or perfect.

- Nurture creativity, self-expression, spontaneity, and lightness. Inject humor into all you do.

- Become more receptive and less active. Allow for more peace and serenity and less effort and self-control.

- Release your need to feel responsible for enacting improvements in the world, sure in the knowledge that larger forces are at work to ensure the best outcomes without your efforts.

- Understand that problems, mistakes, and challenges can be exactly the right teachers we all need to grow.

"We cannot change anything unless we accept it." —C. G. Jung

The Type 1 Virtue

Serenity is the virtue that provides an antidote to the passion of anger for Type 1. In serenity, this type experiences calmness and an absence of tension. When this type sees how their anger puts them at odds with the natural rhythm of life and their own deepest knowing, they consciously shift from resisting reality to accepting "what is." This means happily letting go of their constant vigilance and judging. This, in turn, allows them to surrender to the inherent peace that lies in flowing with life without judging or rejecting or devaluing whatever unfolds in the moment.

If you identify with this type, serenity helps you to lessen the experience of anger in your life, allowing you to let go of your habit of measuring everything against an ideal of perfection. When you release your tendency to judge, you create space for a deep feeling of tranquility that comes with being in harmony with truth—both internally and externally. In serenity, you operate from a perspective you may not have considered before—the perspective of the heart rather than one based on judgment and cultural conditioning.

In the state of serenity you experience:

- Openness, receptivity, and acceptance.

- The inner peace and lightness that occur when the internal dialogue of your inner critic stops.

- An acceptance of reality exactly as it is.

- A sense of emotional and physical relaxation, with fewer concerns than before.

- A tranquil inner atmosphere, free of reactive opposition.

- An inner calm, spontaneity, and contentedness.

- An inner attitude based on the clear recognition that standing against anything blocks you from the flow of life force.

- Full and unconditional emotional acceptance of yourself and others, in gratitude.

- An absence of any kind of agitation, tension, or upset.

- -

"Try to manage your anger, since people can't manage their stupidity." —Nishan Panwar

- -

Waking Up from the Zombie State

For Type 1, the key to embracing the true self lies in gradually learning that, at the level of the false self, they will never approach perfection. But when this type transcends their egos, "good and bad" and "right and wrong" don't make sense anymore. When they achieve the higher state of awareness found in serenity, their true selves rise above their false selves and they learn to trust in the inherent virtue of all beings.

When Type 1s come to see that their focus on getting things right and working relentlessly to meet high standards doesn't ever end in a lasting feeling of satisfaction but only creates more and more stress, they move beyond their fixation on an elusive and illusory ideal. They finally experience the relief of letting go of their need for perfection and their compulsion to judge. And it is here that they find that feeling of liberation that allows them to be light, humorous, fun-loving, and spontaneous.

The Type 1 pathway can be challenging because of the difficulty of releasing the need to do and be right. This moral imperative makes this type feel that they have no choice but to achieve perfection, especially if they equate being flawless with being worthy of love. But when they break out of their limiting habits and embrace the reality that they are already worthy, they no longer have to strive for self-improvement.

As a Type 1, when you start to embody more of your true self, you are carried by the flow of your own natural impulses, instincts, and emotions. You liberate yourself from the constant monitoring of your inner critic and accept *all* of who you are. You begin to channel the energy of anger into achieving positive change in the world. You recognize the purity of your own good intentions and accept your own inherent worthiness. As you rise above your unconscious zombie tendencies of fixating on improvement and repressing your true feelings and desires, you liberate your energies and realize your essential unity with nature. The space that was filled up by the requirements of your inner critic then becomes permeated with a lasting sense of peace, freedom, and joy.

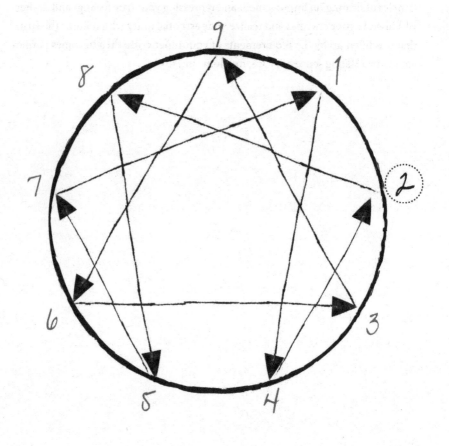

The Path from Pride to Humility

Never believe that a few caring people can't change the world.
For, indeed, that's all who ever have.

MARGARET MEAD

Once upon a time, there was a person named Two. When she was young, she was a happy child, full of love and a deep sense of satisfaction in life. She loved people—and loved loving people. She felt a deep sense of love for herself and all the beings in the world. From birth, she had a beautiful emotional sensitivity and an especially strong need to feel loved and supported.

But as Two grew up, perhaps because of this trait, she experienced bad feelings when some of her needs weren't met by the people around her. Sometimes when she was hungry, no one came to feed her. Sometimes when she got hurt, no one realized she needed comfort. And when she felt her deep need for love, she often felt that she did not receive it.

Two tried to find the love she needed by expressing love for the people around her. She tried to get them to take care of her by taking care of them. If she was very pleasing, helpful, and supportive of others, she thought, they would want to be very pleasing, helpful, and supportive of her. They might remember to take care of her.

To get the love she needed so much, Two found herself doing all she could to please the people in her world. The affection of others made her feel safe and helped her avoid feeling neglected. In her quest to be loved—or liked—she focused a great deal of energy on all her relationships. She created very positive connections with others. She listened to them. She expressed interest in them. She said funny things to entertain them. She always looked her best to impress them. She made them feel happy by giving them things they liked or needed—sometimes even before they knew they needed them. Two became quite good at pleasing people and even liked to do it most of the time, although it sometimes made her very tired.

Over time, Two's desire to win people's love made her extremely good at tuning in to what they were feeling. This helped her make them feel good so they would appreciate her and take care of her. She became very generous and giving because she saw that, when she gave people things, they liked her more. But she didn't like to ask for anything for herself, because others might say "no," and when that happened, she felt rejected. And feeling rejected was the opposite of feeling loved. Eventually, after years of trying to avoid the pain of not being loved, Two erased the memory of love almost completely.

Because Two was so good at doing things that pleased others, a lot of people *did* like her, and this made her feel important. But in focusing on everyone else's needs, Two forgot all about her own needs—and sometimes her feelings. Eventually, she lost all awareness of her needs and feelings. All she ever did was seek approval from others. Driven by her unconscious need to be appreciated, she even started to control and manipulate others, because sometimes she had to *make* them see how important she was. She became really good at imposing her will on others in ways they didn't realize, because she disguised herself so well as a nice, generous, and selfless person.

Two's survival strategies came to rule her life. She completely forgot about the original need for love that had driven her to please others. She sometimes felt a vague sense of satisfaction when they approved of her, but it went away quickly, leaving her even hungrier for more. She tried to meet everyone's needs, even when she was completely exhausted. She shape-shifted into a different person every time she wanted someone's approval and she couldn't say "no" to anyone. Her need to be liked and important became insatiable, and in trying to be whatever she had to be to get people to like her, she lost all memory of her true self.

Occasionally, when someone did offer Two genuine love, she didn't even realize it was happening. By learning to settle for small bits of attention, appreciation, and approval, she had deadened herself to her own larger needs and deeper feelings—and cut herself off from her self and her ability to receive what she wanted the most. This made her totally unable to take in anything good from others, including the love she had wanted in the first place.

Two had become a zombie—a very friendly, generous, helpful zombie, but a zombie just the same.

THE TYPE 2 CHECKLIST

If most or all of the following personality traits apply to you, you may be a Type 2 personality:

- ☑ You focus much of your attention on relationships and how others respond to you.

- ☑ You worry about whether others like you or approve of you.

- ☑ You tune in to the people around you to sense how they feel and what they like, and then shape-shift to align with them and create positive rapport.

- ☑ You habitually anticipate what others may need, especially those who are important to you.

- ☑ You have a difficult time knowing what you need and find it hard to ask for help.

- ☑ You want to be liked by others and to be important to the people who are central in your life.

- ☑ You make positive connections with others, but are very selective when choosing those you want to be close to. Although you want everyone to like you, some people are more important to you than others.

☑ You believe you can make others like you through charm or generosity or support.

☑ You specialize in being friendly, upbeat, and positive, and you take pride in being someone on whom people can count.

If, after using this checklist, you find that you are a Type 2, your growth journey will follow three steps.

First, you will embark on a quest to know yourself by learning to identify personality patterns that focus on becoming whoever you need to be to get people to like you.

Then you must face your Shadow by becoming more aware of how you lose touch with yourself when you accommodate so many different people. This will encourage you to recognize and own ego patterns that aren't so positive and "nice."

The final stage of your journey involves letting go of your false self and owning more of your true self, thus learning to receive the love you seek by living more authentically.

"One does not become enlightened by imagining figures of light, but by making the darkness conscious." —Carl Jung

Embarking on the Quest

For Type 2s, the first stage of awakening involves actively and consciously observing how they tune in to others' feelings more than their own. When they intentionally watch their habitual patterns in action—like how they please others to get something from them while trying to appear selfless and altruistic—they initiate their own awakening.

As a Type 2, your journey starts with developing the capacity to recognize how much attention you give to others and how little attention you pay to your own priorities—without judging yourself. This helps you become aware of all the ways you rely on the approval of others to inform your sense of who you are.

Key Type 2 Patterns

When this type remains unaware of their deep need for love and approval, they think that they support others out of a sincere intention to be of service. But while this may be true some of the time, the truth is that their need to feel important often fuels efforts to exert control to get what they want without asking for it directly. It can be hard to admit this and they may fight against accepting it, but the Type 2 survival strategy often drives this type to try to control or manipulate others, even if they don't see it this way. Being the "savior" often functions as a safe position from which to engage in relationships in that it offers a way to feel important while also avoiding vulnerable feelings. To make progress on their journey, however, 2s must learn to acknowledge this.

If you identify as a Type 2, you must observe and make more conscious these five habitual patterns to move forward on your growth journey.

Needing to Be Liked

Much of the time, you tend to be motivated by approval and have an underlying fear of being rejected or excluded. It's very important to you to be liked by others—and you have the sense you can make others like you. Notice if you worry about the impact you have on people, because it's so important to make a positive impression. Observe yourself to be more conscious of your tendency to "shape-shift" to align with others, presenting yourself in ways you think they will like and hiding parts of yourself you think they won't—your opinions, your preferences, and your feelings.

Minimizing Needs While Seeking to Please Others

You may fear that if you express your needs openly, others will see you as overly "needy." Notice if you feel vulnerable when someone declines to meet your needs, because it feels like rejection and reminds you of the pain of being deprived. Check to see if you often have no idea what you need and, even if you do, you have a hard time asking for it. Most likely it can be difficult or impossible for you to ask for help. You tend to settle for less than what you really need and want, and you prioritize pleasing others over fulfilling your own needs. Without fully realizing it, you may believe that being appreciated for what you do for others is the only way you can get satisfaction in life, while you remain unaware of your own true needs and desires.

Focusing on Relationships

Notice how much attention you focus on relationships. Observe yourself to see if you unconsciously try to get your needs met indirectly through your connections with others. Watch to see if you avoid asking for what you need directly, often fearing you may burden others and drive them away. Without realizing it, you may tend to view interactions as a reciprocal exchange: "If I give you something, you should give me something in return." This "exchange mentality" results in a pattern of over-giving in the hope that you will receive something back without having to ask. This pattern can lead you to feel exhausted and resentful.

Wanting to Feel Important

Notice if you tend to feel driven to impress or please the most important people in your life. You may notice that you expend a lot of energy on earning the affection of people you value, and this need to be important may frequently leave you feeling "not important enough." In your quest to please others and create positive connections, observe yourself to see if you focus your attention on how you may fall short of gaining the approval or importance you want. Notice how you rely on the approval of others to confirm your own sense of self-worth, which can keep you from feeling "okay" about yourself if people disapprove of you in any way. This can drive you to even greater efforts to feel important.

Feeling Pride in Being Needed

Notice if feel a need to play a central role in other people's lives and may not recognize all the things you do to assert your significance to those closest to you. Do you feel a special thrill when someone tells you: "We couldn't have done it without you." You likely tend to ignore or deny all the strategies you employ to offer help and support to others as a way of reminding them that they need you. And while it may be hard to admit, you may tend to become controlling or manipulative when people don't appreciate you (or your guidance) enough or prioritize you after you have met their needs.

. . . .
"Sometimes asking for help is the most meaningful example of self-reliance." —Cory Booker
. . . .

The Type 2 Passion

Pride is the passion that drives Type 2. In this context, pride is a kind of ego inflation—a need to be important or valued. For this type, pride takes on the character of a kind of false arrogance—the kind of pride that caused the mythic "fall" of Satan in the archetypal Christian story. This causes them to "play God" by controlling what happens because they think they know what's best or what should happen. This maintains the illusion that they can direct what happens and how people feel—and that they are not subject to forces beyond their control.

In everyday life, pride leads this type to believe they must be superhuman to be accepted by others. It drives them to meet everyone's needs all the time and to become indispensable. But it also blocks them from being aware of what they need from others and convinces them that they can be all things to all people without needing support. By seeing others' needs but not their own, they unconsciously elevate themselves above everyone else.

This pride—which usually operates outside of conscious awareness—fuels a kind of grandiosity that underlies this type's need to be important. It leads them to deploy support as a form of influence or control. Conversely, they often feel that they can never be good or central enough. In order to grow, they must become aware of both of these manifestations of pride—as the drive to elevate their own importance and as the pain they feel at not being important enough—in order to move forward on their path.

If you identify with Type 2, you must learn to recognize and make conscious these typical manifestations of pride in order to move toward awakening:

- Denying your own needs and fearing that others may perceive you as excessively needy.

- Not asking for help.

- Believing you can meet everyone else's needs, while not admitting your own. Meeting others' needs all the time and feeling resentful when others don't reciprocate by meeting yours.

- Assuming you can make everyone like you.

- Trying to be indispensable by working hard and being competent, generous, and self-sacrificing.

- "Giving to get"—strategically giving to others to earn their approval or support, while denying that you want to get something back.

- Elevating yourself in your own mind; thinking you know best or should be valued as important; being offended when you are not prioritized or central enough.

- Feeling very deflated, disappointed, or insulted when you are criticized, disliked, or not appreciated.

- Positioning yourself as caretaker, rescuer, all-powerful supporter, or the "power behind the throne."

· ·

"Pride erects a little kingdom of its own, and acts as sovereign in it." —William Hazlitt

· ·

Using Type 2 Wings as Growth Stretches

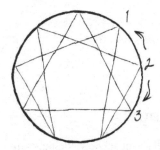

The two personality types adjacent to Type 2 on the Enneagram circle are Types 1 and 3. This type can moderate their excessive focus on getting others' love and attention by "leaning into" Type 1's balance and self-discipline, and then integrating Type 3's ability to set goals and work toward them. This helps them move beyond putting so much attention on relationships and allows them to acknowledge their own needs and priorities.

- First, adopt Type 1's ability to pay more attention to processes, tasks, and outcomes related to improving some aspect of your life or your self-care. Balance your focus on people and relationships with more attention to self-discipline, structure, and supportive routines. When you get overly emotional, practice developing discernment—logically assess what's "right" or "appropriate" in what's happening. When you "lose yourself" by focusing on others, try a step-by-step approach to connect to and fulfill your own personal agenda. Get more grounded in your body by instituting a regular exercise routine or by breathing into your belly the next time you feel ovewhelmed by emotions.

- Then integrate the healthy qualities of Type 3 by focusing more on doing than feeling, detaching from moods and increasing productivity, and setting personal goals and charting a path to meet them. When relationship problems slow you down, concentrate on plowing through your to-do list or just getting the next thing done. When you feel down or depleted, engage in work or activities you enjoy or that satisfy a specific need or desire. Balance your focus on others with more attention to projects and aspirations that benefit you and meet your personal or professional needs.

"We must let go of the life we have planned, so as to accept the one that is waiting for us." —Joseph Campbell

Facing the Shadow

The second part of the Type 2 growth journey is all about acknowledging, owning, and embracing their authentic selves—especially their true needs and emotions—instead of being dominated by matching an image of what others need or want them to be. This helps them see the parts of themselves they have been suppressing or denying and allows them to become more aware that pleasing and caring for others can sometimes be a bad thing.

When this type lacks self-awareness, they can be invasive, needy, and manipulative, even while they consciously think they are being unselfish, independent, and helpful. When they don't confront their innate strategy of giving to get, they can become clingy, hypersensitive, and overly attached to specific relationships or the repayment of perceived debts. When others don't fulfill their unexpressed expectations, they can become quietly resentful or righteously angry. Becoming conscious of this deeper level of motivations and emotional reactivity underneath their pleasant exterior can be painful and even humiliating for them.

Meeting the Type 2 Shadow

If you identify as a Type 2, here are some actions you can take to bring to the surface, become more aware of, and start to counteract the key unconscious patterns, blind spots, and pain points of the type:

- Identify and voice your deeper needs and ask others for help. This may feel very challenging at first, and you may have no idea what you actually need, much less how to ask for it. It may feel humiliating. If it does, see this as a good thing and don't let the sensation of feeling vulnerable stop you.

- Connect with, process, accept, and then manage your emotions. As a Type 2, you can be very emotional, but you also tend to repress your emotions when you fear that they will prevent you from connecting with others.

- Focus less on relationships and being liked. Actively acknowledge that not everyone will like you. While this may seem hard at first, consider how free you will feel when you no longer must present yourself in a way that people will like.

- Let go of relationships that don't serve you. You may tolerate some people longer than you should as you get into the habit of being the supporter and taking pride in being counted on—even when you don't get much back.

- Establish boundaries between you and others; state your wishes and learn to say "no." You will benefit enormously from learning to respect your boundaries and then helping others learn to respect them as well.

Tell people when you don't have time or when what they ask of you is too much.

- Learn what it means to "be yourself." Focus on being authentic and not shape-shifting to please others. Spend time by yourself. Ask yourself what you need, what you want, and what you like—then give it to yourself.

- Feel the freedom of being less important and doing less for others. As you become more conscious of how your need to be important drives you, start to let it go. Be important to yourself just because you're you. Actively appreciate what this freedom feels like.

- Be conscious of your human weaknesses and limitations. Notice when you carry more than your share of the load in relationships and stop doing so much. Just acknowledge and let go of the need to work so hard to earn love.

- Become aware of the accumulated repressed pain from your past and allow yourself to feel sad and brokenhearted. Let yourself feel all the pain, sadness, anger, and whatever other emotions you have likely been avoiding. Let your tears flow. You need this, and it's good for you. And make sure you ask for help to do this.

Your zombie self wants nothing to do with these challenges—especially as you have invested so much in creating and believing in your image of indispensability.

. . . .

"There is no coming to consciousness without pain." —C. G. Jung

. . . .

The Type 2 Blind Spots

This type may not want to acknowledge their blind spots because they tend to be happy—and don't want to feel sad. They may be insecure underneath, but their survival strategies help them avoid the deeper emotions behind their positive outlook and "can do" attitude. They resist looking inward by focusing on earning the "positive" affirmation they seek externally. In feeling proud of being generous and supportive, they ignore what lies beneath their desire to be benevolent—and this blocks their growth.

But here's the good news. If you identify as a Type 2 and are willing to examine your blind spots and feel any pain that arises, you will eventually experience freedom. If you can endure some humiliation when your unconscious relational tactics are exposed, you will feel relieved at not having to do and be so much for others all the time. Here are some habitual unconscious tendencies you must confront to achieve this.

Denying Your Needs

Do you go blank when someone asks what you need? Even if you manage to know what you need, do you have a hard time asking for it? Try these techniques for integrating this blind spot:

- Several times a day, repeat this phrase: "What do I need right now?"

- With a psychotherapist or close friend you trust, talk about all the ways your needs were not met throughout your life. What blocks you from experiencing your needs? What do you fear will happen if you feel or express your needs? What is so bad about appearing needy to others? How do you really feel about people who are needy?

- Get in touch with the pride you feel when you put yourself above others who have needs when you don't. Move toward humility by admitting that you have lots of needs, then name them.

- Become more aware of the fear of rejection that lies behind denying your needs and not asking for help.

- Ask others clearly and directly for what you need. Notice and tolerate the feelings that arise in you when they meet your needs and when they don't.

Giving to Get

Are you aware of the hidden strategies you employ when you help others? Do you deny exactly what you want to get when you offer support? Does offering "strategic help" to others function as an attempt to fill your unmet need for love? Here are some actions you can take to integrate this blind spot:

- Recognize your underlying motives every time you offer help or support to someone. What do you want in return?

- Become aware of the resentment you feel when you don't get what you want after you've done someone a favor—even when you didn't realize you wanted it.

- Be aware of any desire to manipulate people or situations. What do you see yourself doing that could be called "manipulation"? How do you try to get what you want indirectly? What stops you from communicating what you need more directly?

- Admit that you may not be as helpful as you may seem and that you sometimes use helpfulness as a vehicle for getting something for yourself.

- Become aware of your fear that someone will refuse if you ask for help. What feelings are you avoiding by not asking for what you need?

- Notice that praising, pleasing, flattering, or supporting others are all methods by which you try to get people to like or love you. Make your unmet need for love and care more conscious.

Fearing and Avoiding Intimacy

Do you feel fear when someone gets close to you and actually becomes available to love you? Does it feel challenging to take in positive feedback from others? Do you have difficulty internalizing and making use of the good things that do come to you? Do you struggle to truly allow people to get close to you? Ironically, Type 2 has a hard time letting in the love they seek. Here are some things you can do to integrate this blind spot:

- Recognize how difficult it is to receive the love you want and try so hard to get. Notice that even when you successfully charm others, you have a difficult time accepting affection.

- Acknowledge how hard it is for you to receive a compliment. Try to understand what stands in your way of receiving the positive affirmation you seek. Work on actively taking in positive feedback.

- Observe your tendency to need more appreciation, no matter how much you get.

- Explore why you focus on getting love from unavailable people. Learn how you are activated by challenging relationships and why you pursue people who can't meet your needs as a way to avoid intimacy.

- Get in touch with your fear of real contact by investigating what happens when someone who can love you comes close to you. Work to understand the sources and shape of this fear. Speak about your fear or discomfort with someone to whom you want to be closer as a way of allowing for more intimacy.

- Do "mirror work"; practice saying positive affirmations to yourself in front of a mirror and letting them land inside you.

. . . .
"To be alive is to be vulnerable."
—Madeleine L'Engle
. . . .

Type 2 Pain

This type tends to be happy and cheerful. They focus on positive emotions as part of their compulsion to make others feel good. They also tend to repress or unconsciously avoid painful feelings like anger, sadness, or hurt. They often subconsciously worry that, if they express "negative" emotions, others will not like them. They notice that others like happy people and complain about those who are moody or overly emotional. So they adopt the emotional mood-state they think will attract others and avoid being in touch with their true emotions in an attempt to maintain harmony in their relationships.

In order to awaken, Type 2s must become more aware of their real emotions, feel them fully, accept them, and stop being embarrassed about them. They are naturally emotional people, and their feelings bring important information to them. But they actively push away feelings they don't feel comfortable showing, or that they fear will make others uncomfortable. To grow, this type needs to welcome all their feelings—including their pain. Just like all of us, they can awaken the zombie only by feeling their pain.

If you identify with Type 2, you may find it difficult to confront the fact that not everyone likes you as much as you want them to, or that perhaps not everyone welcomes your "help." Here are some techniques that can support you in learning to tolerate these specific painful feelings and allow for a fuller realization of your true self:

- Get in touch with any fear you may have that your personality tendencies and tactics will be exposed. Confront the illusion that you can manage the impressions you make and let your relationships play out. It can be humiliating to realize that your strategies are just desperate attempts to get people to love you. Learn to be honest about your mistakes, your inauthenticity, your pride, and other flaws. Realize that your need for affirmation sometimes leads you to be manipulative, controlling, pushy, invasive, or intrusive.

- Recognize the exhaustion you feel when you finally allow yourself to admit how much you do for others.

- Learn to acknowledge the anger you feel at not being "seen," appreciated, understood, or loved. Notice the resentment you feel when you don't receive what you think you deserve—or when you realize you have abandoned yourself in order to focus on others. Have the courage to discern when this is legitimate anger or resentment, and when it comes from pride.

- Feel into and accept the pain you experience when people don't like or love you as much as you want or need them to. Learn to deal with the pain that comes from feeling misunderstood, rejected, not heard, or excluded.

- Find ways to cope with the confusion that comes from not having a clear sense of yourself—not knowing who you are—after you have spent so much time trying to be what others want you to be. You may feel lost because you have "shape-shifted" to please others.

- Be open to the sadness you feel at not being loved for who you really are—and the grief for having "lost yourself" in your efforts to evoke affection. Own the sadness you feel for abandoning yourself in the search for love, as well as the sadness grounded in your need to get approval, when what you really want and need is love.

. . . .

"Love seeks one thing only: the good of the one loved.
It leaves all the other secondary effects to take care of
themselves. Love, therefore, is its own reward."
—Thomas Merton

. . . .

The Type 2 Subtypes

Identifying your Type 2 subtype can help you target your efforts to confront your blind spots, unconscious tendencies, and hidden pain. The specific patterns and tendencies of the subtypes vary depending on which of the three survival instincts dominates your experience.

Self-Preservation 2 Subtype

This subtype is more childlike, and more fearful and shy, than other Type 2 subtypes. They appear charming, youthful, and playful, but are also more sensitive to being hurt. They are more ambivalent about connecting with others and focus on creating rapport, but they may also withdraw when hurt or reluctant to commit. They crave freedom the most. They exhibit a mixture of high competence and periodic bouts of helplessness. They can be driven and hard-working, but are occasionally lazy, overwhelmed, self-indulgent, anxious, or needy.

Social 2 Subtype

This subtype shows more leadership characteristics than the other two. They focus more on power and influence and so have a need to "seduce" groups. They project competence and confidence, and are good at playing to the crowd. They tend to enjoy public speaking. They are the most apt to give strategically to get something back. They are more politically savvy, but find it hard to be vulnerable. They tend more to deny their own needs and hesitate to ask for help directly. This is the most controlling of the three subtypes, and they display more of a tendency to manipulate to get what they want.

Sexual (One-to-One) 2 Subtype

This subtype focuses the most attention on one-to-one relationships. They present themselves as perfect partners and work to make romantic connections happen with a lot of intensity. They take pride in being attractive, appealing, and exciting partners. They are good at flirting and communicating openness to connection. They express generosity and devotion as a way of seducing others into relationship. They react most aggressively when rejected. They may use sexuality as a weapon and experience intense anguish when an important relationship ends.

The Type 2 Subtype Shadows

You can more effectively confront your own Shadow if you know the specific shadow characteristics of your Type 2 subtype. Below are some of the shadow aspects of each subtype. As subtype behavior can be highly automatic, these traits can be hardest to see and own.

Self-Preservation 2 Shadow

If this is your subtype, you sometimes adopt a childish attitude, throwing tantrums or sulking instead of growing up and engaging in life in a mature way. Hiding or withdrawing are your key modes of defense. You "play small" as a fearful reaction to the self-elevating tendency of pride. You take refuge in helplessness or hopelessness as a defense against showing up in life, opening up to people, or doing impactful work. You may consider yourself independent, but also maintain unconscious dependencies. You can tend to get stuck in resentment, fear, or anxiety to avoid taking responsibility and stepping into your power.

Social 2 Shadow

If this is your subtype, you tend to remain blind to pride and the way it fuels a need for importance and power. It will be important to notice if you display helpfulness and generosity as a strategy to exert control or gain influence. You may support others as a means to control or manipulate. You may get angry when others reject your advice or your help. You appear warm and magnanimous, but can be ruthless when seeking power or exerting control. You avoid vulnerable feelings, but may deploy a (false) vulnerable persona as part of an effort to seduce. You repress exhaustion and sadness in order to serve the ego's need to be powerful and influential.

Sexual (One-to-One) 2 Shadow

If this is your subtype, you may display false generosity in order to seduce. Notice if you flirt to draw others in, but may not always follow through on your promises. You take pride in being the "special one"—the perfect partner or lover—and can use sex as a weapon of conquest. You may even exhibit vampiric tendencies, engineering relationships through an attractive presentation and then demanding that partners give you everything you want and need. You tend to react aggressively when seduction fails or your needs are not met. You may exhibit anxiety when you are without a partner to provide external affirmation. Breakups can feel like death to you because your sense of self gets lost in merging with the other.

. . . .

> "Someday, when I manage to finally figure out how to take care of myself, then I'll consider taking care of someone else."
> —Marilyn Manson

. . . .

The Type 2 Paradox

The Type 2 paradox can be experienced in the polarity between the passion of pride and the virtue of humility. Humility is a state of being totally at peace with staying exactly who you are—no more or no less—and just as important as you inherently are. This type needs to recognize the need they have to be seen positively and to be important to others. By becoming more aware of how their pride operates, they get to know and accept themselves as they are, and stop trying to fit an inflated image of how they would like others to see them.

If you identify with this type, here are some first steps you can take toward becoming more conscious of your pride:

- Recognize when you feel a need to be superhuman. Allow yourself to relax and just be who you are. Let go of your desire for recognition and do things anonymously, without worrying about getting the credit.

- Notice when you act from pride without judging yourself. Ask yourself what is most real and vulnerable in you in the present moment. Express that vulnerability and see failures as opportunities for humility.

- Have compassion for the part of you that needs to feel important to others to affirm your self-worth and be lovable. Allow yourself to feel the pain of not always getting the love you want, and not being the person you think you should be to be loved.

- Consider whether, in reaction to the impulse to be important, you make yourself *less important* than you actually are. Become aware of how you feel when you want to be important and something or someone tells you you're not. Learn to own your actual level of importance.

- Honor the exhaustion you feel when you over-give or over-empathize, and register the relief you experience when you say "no" or stop supporting others and just focus on yourself.

- Get in touch with your specific needs and allow yourself to feel and accept them as ordinary, normal human needs. See the pride in not speaking your needs. Ask for help several times a day.

. . . .

"Pride is spiritual cancer: it eats up the very possibility of
love, or contentment, or even common sense."
—C. S. Lewis

. . . .

Using Type 2 Arrow Lines for Growth

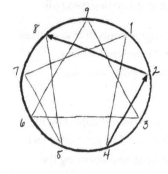

The two personality types connected to Type 2 by the internal arrow lines of the Enneagram diagram are Types 4 and 8. This type can experience a radical growth shift and move beyond their usual focus on people and relationships by developing Type 4's ability to access needs and emotions, and then integrating Type 8's capacity for constructive conflict. This helps them see beyond shape-shifting to connect with people and acknowledge their own needs and feelings.

- First, adopt Type 4's ability to express needs and accept authentic emotions. Pay more attention to what's going on inside you. Balance your external focus on what's good for others with attention to your own emotions, desires, and preferences. Learn to feel, accept, and get comfortable with all your emotions. Develop more ease and confidence in communicating your feelings to others. Get to know who you really are and convey your truth to others through some form of authentic self-expression. Learn to be more real and name what's true more fearlessly.

- Then integrate Type 8's ability to confront challenges. After you get more grounded in an appreciation of your inner territory and natural sensitivity by working with the healthy aspects of Type 4, develop your ability to say what you think, ask for what you want, and step into your power and authority. Be more direct, assertive, and honest. Care less about others' approval, and develop more self-confidence and a thicker skin. Own your power and strength and step into your true authority. State your authentic opinion and don't apologize as much. Learn to communicate anger in healthy ways and engage in constructive conflicts that strengthen your relationships.

"Humility is nothing but truth, and pride is nothing but lying." —St. Vincent de Paul

EMBRACING THE HIGH SIDE

On the third part of their journey, Type 2s begin to see more clearly who they are *not* and stops creating an identity based on who others want them to be. When they consciously work to become more self-aware, understand their blind spots, and face their pain, they experience the freedom of not depending on others to affirm their self-worth.

The challenge for this type is that they must wake up and learn to value themselves by getting to know themselves. When they do, they stop needing to earn love or do something for others as a way of being affirmed by the outside world. They become conscious of their pride and the needs that drive them, and learn that life is better when they abandon their desire to control. They learn to relax into the happiness and peace that come from knowing their own worth. They find that, by cultivating the humility that come from knowing, liking, and accepting themselves exactly as they are, they no longer need to exhaust themselves trying to please others.

This higher state of consciousness can only be attained by doing the hard work required—work that allows for the development of a greater ability to experience love, unity, and connection with others and the universe. Type 2s experience this as a state in which the ego's need for superiority or outsized importance makes no sense. This means that they stop comparing themselves to others, relinquish their need to be indispensable, and cease striving for attention.

If you identify as a Type 2, here are some things you will be able to do in this higher state that you couldn't do before:

- Help others with no expectation of reciprocity. Regularly experience the sense of joy that comes from giving from a place of pure love—and only if you are called to do so.

- Be who you are with no apologies and no concerns about whether people approve of you—even the most important people.

- Express your needs, feelings, and desires freely and openly. Trust that the universe will take care of you.

- Stop apologizing for or regretting any perceived negative impact you may have on others. Trust others to take care of themselves more and investigate whether they really need your help.

- Trust yourself more and stop doubting your value or second-guessing yourself.

- Be in touch with pain and suffering from your past and more humbly in touch with your heart.

- Own any mistakes you make and be less concerned with how people see you.

- Welcome the experience of being only as important as you are—and not less so. Acknowledge that what needs to happen will happen, without you getting involved.

- Love yourself for who you are and find affirmation within. Own your inherent goodness, knowing that you have nothing to prove or earn.

. . . .

"Pride makes us artificial. Humility makes us real."
—Thomas Merton

. . . .

The Type 2 Virtue

The Type 2 virtue of humility opposes the passion of pride. Humility gives this type a clear goal to work toward after acknowledging their habitual patterns that stem from pride and the search for love. By working against the tendencies fueled by pride and trying to embody the qualities of humility, they wake up and move closer to their real selves.

If you identify as a Type 2, humility means that you no longer need to be superhuman to have value. It means not making yourself more important than you actually are—or less important. It means having a realistic sense of exactly who you are and who you are not—and feeling joy, peace, and satisfaction in your authentic self. It means loving yourself just because you are you, and allowing others to do the same. Here are some other positive traits you will acquire as you move toward accessing your higher side through being more in touch with the virtue of humility:

- Not needing to feel important.

- Knowing yourself, liking yourself, and feeling at peace with exactly who you are and how important you actually are.

- Giving to others generously and anonymously, without expectation of reward. Not needing to be recognized or acknowledged for the good things you do.

- Understanding that not everyone will like you and being okay with that—even welcoming it.

- Being completely honest with yourself and others about your needs, feelings, and limitations.

- Asking for help and being open to receiving it. Opening up to love, knowing (and being happy that) you can't control how people see you and feel about you.

- Establishing boundaries, saying "no," and caring for yourself.

- Feeling good about yourself because of your true worth, whether or not others approve of you or affirm you.

. . . .
"Only a person who has passed through the gate of humility can ascend to the heights of the spirit." —Rudolf Steiner
. . . .

Waking Up from the Zombie State

For Type 2s, the key to embracing their true selves lies in gradually learning to love themselves. This can seem difficult, if not impossible, early in their journey, because their egos tell them that they are "not enough," that they "need to do more," that they aren't attractive, competent, or perfect enough to be loved. When they face their personality patterns and their pain, however, they rise above the limiting definitions of the past and achieve a higher degree of self-knowledge and self-respect, as well as a wider vision of who they are.

When this type realizes that relying on others to determine their own worth just doesn't work and never allows for a real experience of love, they can begin to focus all their intention and attention on loving themselves. And it is only when they love themselves that they can feel love for others or fully feel another's love. In zombie mode, this type trades in fake love. When they wake up, they become capable of real love—for themselves and for others. When they understand this, they free themselves to be—and to love—who they are. This causes them to become generous, humble, warm, independent-minded, and direct.

The Type 2 path can be challenging because of the tricky nature of pride and our natural resistance to feeling hurt, pain, grief, and humiliation. In some contexts, pride is a good thing. But pride can secretly keep Type 2s attached to a deep need to control how people feel about them. It can cause them to maintain a "positive" view of themselves in the world and in their own minds, while also hiding many of the problematic effects of this need. When they courageously and compassionately face their Shadow and own the difficult emotions they need to feel to break free from the constraints of their nice-seeming personality, they gain true freedom.

Even before taking this journey, this type often feels a deep craving to feel more free. This makes sense, given that their main survival strategy relies on pleasing and supporting others, which compels them to trade liberty for approval. But as they begin to liberate themselves from the need to be validated by the outside world, they come to know their inherent goodness and lovability, and awaken to a more authentic sense of being grounded in who they really are.

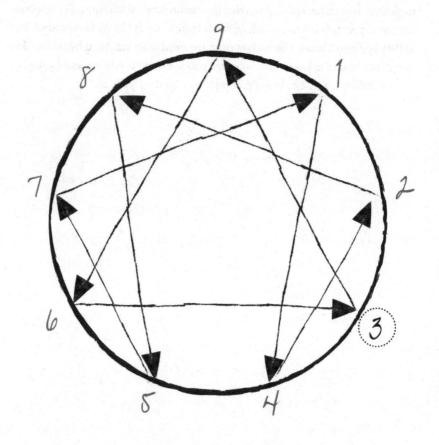

The Path from Self-Deceit to Veracity

Some liars are so expert they deceive themselves.
Those who believe it is all right to tell little white lies soon grow color blind.

AUSTIN O'MALLEY

Once upon a time, there was a person named Three. She came into this world as a naturally emotional child and she was always completely true to her sweet, emotional nature. Everybody could see that she had a very pure and authentic heart.

But early in life, Three saw that she was praised for what she did, not for who she was. Everyone around her got very excited and happy when she successfully completed her homework, or did a trick in gymnastics, or won a game. But when she expressed her true emotions, when she felt sad or disappointed or hurt, no one paid any attention to her at all. She felt lonely and scared when no one recognized her or cared about what she expressed from her heart. People seemed to like her when she accomplished things; but they acted as if she didn't exist when she was just being herself.

Three found a way to make sure that she wouldn't feel alone or fearful anymore. She discovered that she had the ability to sense what people valued and then magically turn herself into exactly that. She was a shape-shifter. When she was around different groups of people, she could become the perfect example of whatever they viewed as admirable or successful. Like a chameleon, she could change her outward appearance depending on whom she was with and the situation she was in. This ability helped her to get attention, which felt good. And it also helped her to avoid being overlooked, which felt bad.

As she grew, Three came to see that others admired those who were successful—who achieved whatever goal they set for themselves. When she earned a lot of money, or won at sports, or looked more attractive than everyone else, people paid attention to her. So Three found that her ability to shape-shift could bring her many rewards in life. By succeeding at being successful, she could attract positive attention, especially because she was willing to do whatever it took to create a really convincing image of whatever others valued.

In fact, Three was so good at being successful that she couldn't stop working and couldn't stop shifting her appearance to promote her success. And she feared that, if she stopped, she wouldn't get the attention and praise she needed. As time went on, she totally lost sight of who she really was beneath all the different images of success she invented, until, eventually, she could no longer feel her real emotions or recognize her real self. She just had to keep moving and working hard to maintain the image of success that made her feel valued. It was *a lot* of work. But, fortunately, Three was really good at doing a lot of work.

Three's survival strategies worked so well that she never even had time to wonder about who she really was. Every once in a while, she felt a momentary wish to be more authentic—to have real contact with the people around her— but this wasn't possible. She had to keep working to make sure that everyone admired her. She couldn't imagine what would happen if she stopped. Unfortunately for Three, her survival strategies brought her too many rewards—money, titles, applause, and attention—for her to give them up.

One morning, Three couldn't get out of bed. She was so weighed down by stress and depression that she remained in bed for two weeks. And that was when she realized, much to her surprise, that she was totally exhausted by all the hard work she did to maintain her image. She finally acknowledged that, deep inside, she was actually very sad and lonely. When Three recovered, however, she forgot all about her sadness and her loneliness, and thought about all the things she had to do at work and all the people she needed to impress. So, with a feeling of relief that she was back in the game—but not many other feelings—she returned to her busy schedule.

Three had become a zombie—a very successful, attractive, and impressive zombie, but a zombie just the same.

THE TYPE 3 CHECKLIST

If most or all of the following personality traits apply to you, you may be a Type 3:

- ☑ You excel at "reading a room"—automatically tuning in to the people around you to know what they value so you can tailor how you present yourself to impress them.

- ☑ You like setting goals and then doing whatever it takes to accomplish them. When you define the result you want, you easily map a path to get there.

- ☑ You want people to see you as competent and successful. You feel confident about your public persona because you do whatever it takes to work hard and deliver.

- ☑ Without even trying, you see what you need to do to appear and be successful in different contexts in your life.

- ☑ You have an easy time accomplishing tasks and enjoy being productive and getting things done. It can be difficult to slow down or stop doing.

- ☑ Although you may not consciously try, you can effectively shift the way you appear to present the right image for every situation.

- ☑ You avoid failure at all costs. If you think you may fail at something, you don't even try to do it.

- ☑ While you value your relationships, they sometimes take a back seat to your work because you so naturally focus on whatever tasks need to get done.

☑ Although you can be very emotional on the inside, you unconsciously avoid expressing your emotions so you can perform.

If, after using this checklist, you identify yourself as a Type 3, your growth journey will follow three steps.

First, you will embark on the quest to know yourself by learning to recognize the ways you shift your identity whenever you need to be viewed as competent, admirable, or successful.

Then you must face your Shadow by realizing that you have lost sight of your true self by adopting different images and roles to appear successful. Only then can you go on to explore the ego patterns that keep you focused on being and looking successful.

The final stage of your journey involves acknowledging your feelings and getting to know who you really are so you can live more from your true identity and allow for real connection with others.

. . . .

"The worst of all deceptions is self-deception."
—Plato

. . . .

EMBARKING ON THE QUEST

As a Type 3, the first part of your awakening involves watching the way you tune in to others and "read" them to know how to present yourself. When you notice how quickly you shift your appearance to evoke admiration, you begin to recognize how much attention you place on completing tasks and looking good, and how little attention you focus on your own inner emotions and your deeper desires. By becoming aware of all the things you do to gain the approval of others (without judging yourself), you activate your ability to self-reflect, opening yourself to a process of reanimation.

Key Type 3 Patterns

Most Type 3s don't question why they work so hard to achieve goals and appear successful. They become addicted to work and have workaholic tendencies. They may have difficulty slowing down or stopping because they have a hard time giving up the rewards that working hard brings, including wealth, status, and a good reputation. And they may have a particularly hard time waking up to their specific "zombie mode" because their habitual patterns get reinforced by a culture that values success. So they need to make a sincere effort to see how they get trapped by their own accomplishments.

If you identify as this type, focus on and make more conscious these five habitual Type 3 patterns to start your journey.

Automatically Shape-Shifting to Impress Others

Observe how you shape-shift naturally and continually to adapt to different people and situations. Notice if, without thinking about it, you read your audience to get a sense of what they value and then "identify with"—or take on the attributes of—the ideal image of what they consider valuable. Watch to see if you tend to remain unaware of the subtle ways in which you shift your persona to match what others view as admirable, and you may confuse this persona with your true self. In light of this tendency, begin to ask yourself who you really are.

Needing to Appear Successful

Notice if you "index" success in the things you do. See if you determine what to do and how to do it by measuring how well it's working in terms of what the people around you define as "success." Observe how you may build an identity around your ability to be successful in everything you do, and redefine yourself in light of that success. Your idea of success tends to be based on your social or work environment and you structure your goals to fit the standards held by others. You probably tend to work hard to accomplish tasks and meet goals—whether in terms of material possessions, status, education, or position. You likely set a fast pace to produce results quickly and efficiently.

Prioritizing Doing Over Feeling

Notice how you focus primarily on getting things done. It can be hard for you to slow down and stop *doing,* and you probably never leave time or space to just *be.* When you observe yourself, you may notice that you find it difficult even to consider slowing down and just being—or feeling. If you try to stop all your activity for a short period of time, it may feel scary and challenging. It can be difficult for you to acknowledge your emotions and you tend to deny or avoid them. You tend to equate who you are with what you do and can feel threatened at the propect of doing less.

Shutting Off Awareness of Emotions

Your emotions are almost always nearby, but you unconsciously fear they will make you less productive. You may have a hard time trusting that you will be loved for who you are (and how you feel) as you may believe that people love you based on what you do. So, you may be motivated to deny or suppress your emotions unconsciously, despite being an intrinsically emotional person. You will especially tend to avoid your emotions when your environment somehow discourages emotional expression. When you disconnect from or avoid your feelings, you disconnect from the truth of who you are.

Avoiding Failure

You probably don't know how to describe failure, because you have never acknowledged experiencing it. If you have experienced failure, you likely simply consider it an important learning opportunity on your journey toward success. You may do everything possible to avoid failure because you fear that it will come to define you. Your need to do and achieve tends to drive your fear of failure, and your aversion to failing may make it difficult for you to stop working and experience more peace—and more of yourself. This can keep you from being available for nurturing relationships.

. . . .

"Awakening is not changing who you are, but discarding who you are not." —Deepak Chopra

. . . .

The Type 3 Passion

Self-deceit is the passion that drives Type 3. In its expression as the core emotional motivation of this type, self-deceit is an unconscious tendency to shape-shift to present themselves in a way others will approve of and admire. This type creates and maintains an ideal image or persona, and then identifies with (or sees themselves as) that persona. This self-deceit is sometimes misunderstood as lying. But most Type 3s don't intentionally deceive people; they just present themselves as something they are not without being aware of who they really are. They automatically appear in ways they think necessary to be accepted or loved, and this can mean that they hide the truth from themselves. Even as children, they sense what their families want them to be, and their attempt to fulfill those expectations is not a conscious process; it's a survival strategy.

Throughout life, this self-deceit fuels this type's need to become whatever they need to be to be valued or admired. Eventually, they come to believe they *are* what they thought they needed to become. This usually happens automatically and unconsciously. Their skill at shape-shifting means they alter their appearance to fit a situation without really thinking about it. They lie to themselves in that they come to believe that they are what they do—or that they are equal to the image they take on to impress others. The self-deceit happens when they buy into this deception instead of realizing they are more than their image. Eventually, they lose sight of who they really are beneath all the shifting and the actions that support it.

If you identify with Type 3, you must observe and make more conscious these typical manifestations of self-deceit to make progress on your path to awakening. It will be important for you to become more aware that it is your self-deceit that fuels these tendencies:

- Being extremely successful, even if you achieve success through doing things you don't really want (or love) to do.

- Concealing aspects of yourself—feelings, ideas, and opinions—that don't conform to the image you try to create.

- Shifting your appearance to meet an ideal of what people value in different social environments.

- Modeling your persona on what you see as ideal according to social consensus. This can lead to mistaking yourself for another Enneagram type.

- Focusing all your energy on doing and achieving rather than just *being* yourself.

- Expressing a high degree of self-confidence that you can meet any goal and accomplish any task.

- Skillfully selling any image or product based on knowing how to package it.

- Thinking you can do any job or adopt any image to gain the admiration of others, no matter how difficult or exhausting.

- Shutting down awareness of your own emotions, fearing they may get in the way of whatever you need to do in service of a specfic image or achievement.

. . . .

"Nothing is easier than self-deceit. For what each man wishes, that he also believes to be true." —Demosthenes

. . . .

Using Type 3 Wings as Growth Stretches

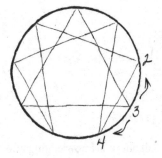

The two types adjacent to Type 3 on the Enneagram circle are Types 2 and 4. This type can begin to move beyond their usual focus on tasks and goals by connecting more deeply with others through accessing Type 2 traits, then intentionally getting more in touch with their emotions by integrating the healthy qualities of Type 4.

- First, adopt Type 2's ability to create rapport with others. Balance your habit of prioritizing tasks with paying more attention to enjoying quality time with the important people in your life. At work, focus less on being productive and efficient, and more on collaborating with and listening to others. Encourage stronger teamwork at home and at work in service of common goals and projects. Try to get more in touch with your own emotions by making more of an effort to empathize with how others feel. Put others' goals above your own and don't get impatient when they share how they feel. Place more emphasis on valuing emotions and relationships.

- Then integrate Type 4 traits by intentionally connecting more deeply with your own emotions. Allow yourself space and time to make contact with how you feel. Learn the value of feeling *all* your feelings, including your pain. Remind yourself that your emotions can be trusted as valid indicators of who you really are and what's important to you. Express yourself more while in touch with these emotions, whether through creative activities or talking openly with others. Make a daily practice of slowing down your work pace and regularly accessing your feelings and desires. Balance your ability to become what people admire with a capacity to know what really matters to you.

Tell the truth, even when that's hard, and live more from a sense of authenticity, meaning, and purpose.

. . . .

"Deception may give us what we want for the present, but it will always take it away in the end." —Rachel Hawthorne

. . . .

FACING THE SHADOW

The second part of the Type 3 growth journey is all about acknowledging and understanding how and why they live their lives focused on creating a false persona while not leaving space for their emotions and other authentic aspects of their true selves. This leads them to discover more about who they truly are and opens the door to living more authentically from their real feelings and sense of purpose.

Relentlessly pursuing the esteem and approval of others can lead to a lack of self-awareness, causing this type to become superficial, inauthentic, and confused about their true character, even while they strive to be effective, praiseworthy, and prosperous. By equating their own worth with their accomplishments, they fall into the trap of denying their own depths. They lose touch with how they feel and who they are, and then act or react only according to their superficial masks. When they lie to themselves and promote a false image without realizing it, they risk becoming empty shells, unable to express real feelings and unavailable for real human connection.

Meeting the Type 3 Shadow

If you identify as a Type 3, here are some actions you can take to bring to the surface, become more aware of, and work to counteract the key unconscious patterns, blind spots, and pain points of this type:

- Slow down your level and pace of "doing." Notice what you feel inside when you slow down or stop.

- Engage in relaxing activities that don't involve goals or tasks. Allow yourself some down time and notice any fear or anxiety that arises.

- Welcome your emotions. Acknowledge how emotional you really are and reframe your feelings as a positive experience.

- Expose all the ways you lie to yourself and investigate the reasons behind illusions that seem necessary.

- Damage your image. Consciously choose to do or say things you like, but that don't add to—or potentially tarnish—your image. Observe who likes you anyway.

- Engage in an activity that holds the possibility of failure. Notice what happens inside you and reframe failure as a positive learning experience.

- Get closer to people who appreciate the "real you." Move away from people who support your false self or reinforce your need to maintain an image that perpetuates a lie.

- Share more of what you really think and feel with the people closest to you.

- Find good mirrors that reflect your real self. Ask three people who know you well to tell you what they like most about you. Is what they say about you or your image?

. . . .

"We cast a shadow on something wherever we stand."
—E. M. Forster

. . . .

The Type 3 Blind Spots

This type may not want to examine their blind spots because they think everything is working well for them. Especially in Western society, they get rewarded for what they do best—produce results and look good. However, they may not know themselves very well at a deeper level—and this may prevent them from feeling fully satisfied in life. But looking inside themselves can seem threatening and scary. Their survival strategies function to keep them working constantly and focused on how competent they appear. They may feel secure in their ability to get things done and believe that they have nothing to gain by examining what they've hidden from themselves in order to do so much. When they refuse to look inside, however, they block their growth.

But here's the good news. If you identify with this type and have the courage to investigate who you *really* are, you will experience a deeper and much richer form of success. If you can endure some disorienting experiences as you search behind your mask, you will gradually be able to feel more fulfillment, freedom, and relief as you learn to live more from your authentic self.

Here are some of the blind spots that most often block Type 3s on their growth journey—and ideas about what to do to make them more conscious.

Doing Too Much

Do you put all your focus on doing without being aware of the negative aspects of maintaining such a high level of activity? Do you find justifications to support being busy all the time? Here are some things you can do to integrate this blind spot:

- Get an objective assessment of your physical and psychological health. Have you been ill or injured in the last few years? Do you really take care of yourself? Allow yourself to become aware of the real risks associated with working so hard.

- Assess your current work-life balance, then get feedback about your assessment. Be honest about what any imbalance may mean and its consequences.

- Recognize that being addicted to work can be just as destructive as being addicted to a substance. Workaholic tendencies can be a sign of unresolved trauma. Find ways to reduce your workload.

- Work with a therapist or a close friend to explore your inner territory and have "secret and sacred" talks about the not-so-good sides of you.

- Consider what you may be missing in your life because of how hard you work. Do you have problems with people because of your workload? Are you missing quality time you will never get back with children, partners, or friends?

- Experiment with slowing down your pace, taking breaks, or sitting and doing nothing. Meditate. Breathe.

Avoiding Emotions

Does your inability to slow down help you avoid experiencing the emotions that might arise if you left more open space in your life? Do you prevent yourself from acknowledging your emotions by refusing to make space for them? Do you suppress or try to outrun your emotions rather than attempt to understand and honor them? Here are some techniques you can use to integrate this blind spot:

- Become more aware of any limiting beliefs that tell you that "you are what you do."

- Acknowledge how confused or fearful you may feel when you begin to access your emotions. Have compassion for yourself as you work to understand them. Ask for support.

- Become actively conscious of any beliefs you hold that cause you to devalue your emotions—for instance, that emotions are unproductive and might hold you back.

- Practice being more aware of your emotions. Keep a journal in which you write about what you feel every day; listen to music or watch movies that evoke emotion.

- When other people share their feelings with you, take the time to listen. Notice if you feel impatient or uncomfortable.

- Practice being present and open when others discuss their emotions or when you experience your own feelings. Reframe exploring all your feelings as a highly positive growth step.

Denying the Value of Failure

Do you place too much value on your accomplishments as a measure of your worth—whether or not they have any intrinsic importance to you? Do you tend to resist seeing how superficial or empty they can be? Do you strive constantly for success and do all you can to avoid failure? Do you remain blind to possibilities and opportunities by not engaging in potentially positive experiences because you believe you won't succeed? Try these techniques to integrate this blind spot:

- Deeply explore how you define success for yourself. Is it based on what others think or on what has meaning for you?

- Notice if, when you succeed at something, you pause for even a moment to celebrate before moving on to the next thing you need to do to be successful.

- Next time you achieve a "win," slow down and take it in. If you immediately want to start running toward your next goal, ask yourself why and consider how you feel about all this striving.

- Ask yourself how meaningful your recent successes have really been to you. Were they things you really wanted to do?

- Notice and list all the things you do in your life to avoid experiencing failure. Why do you work so hard to prevent yourself from failing?

- Consider the ways in which failing might actually be a good thing. List all the possible positive aspects of failure.

. . . .

"The human face is, after all, nothing more nor less than a mask." —Agatha Christie

. . . .

Type 3 Pain

Type 3s tend to be positive, confident people who habitually resist feeling their pain—or feeling any emotions at all. They are sometimes stereotyped as being "unemotional," but this is not true. In fact, they are very emotional beneath the surface. But when they employ their survival strategy of doing rather than feeling, they develop habitual defenses against acknowledging or exploring their emotions.

To proceed on their growth journey, this type must slow down and engage with their emotions and their pain—both past and present. When they leave enough space for their emotions to be felt, they often find they can access them more easily. Once they become aware of how they have unconsciously avoided feeling their emotions, they can interrupt this impulse and start to welcome them. When they begin to feel their pain, they discover that developing awareness of their emotions, while difficult at first, leads them directly to a fuller recognition of their authentic selves.

If you identify with this type, it may be difficult at first for you to make contact with all your emotions, including your pain. You may fear that being emotional will get in the way of working, meeting goals, or maintaining your good image. But fully feeling your emotions is an important step on your particular path to freedom. You must learn to tolerate these specific painful feelings to emerge from your zombie mode and work toward a fuller realization of your true self:

- Confusion that stems from your tendency to shape-shift and see yourself as the persona you create for the outside world. This can keep you from recognizing your true self. When you first get in touch with your feelings, you may feel lost, as if you don't know who you are. You may feel confused about experiencing your emotions, and you may be tempted to continue to avoid them.

- Fear of the unknown and of unfamiliar feelings. You may fear letting go of the identity and sense of control you get from your false self. You may fear that expressing emotions will hurt your image in the eyes of others.

- Embarrassment if you show your emotions in front of others. You may miss the safety you found in the carefully crafted persona you have presented to the world.

- Exhaustion from your efforts. Your newly acknowledged feelings may make you realize how hard you work and how much you do.

- Impatience with others if they push you to feel more than you are ready to feel. Indeed, this reaction may come from your false rather than your true self.

- Sadness that stems from your fears that people may like your image more than you. You may grieve over having spent so much time not knowing that your false self wasn't real. It may sadden you to sense that people don't know the real you—and that you don't either.

. . . .

"In a time of universal deceit, telling the truth is a revolutionary act." —George Orwell

. . . .

The Type 3 Subtypes

Identifying your Type 3 subtype can help you more precisely target your efforts to confront your blind spots, unconscious tendencies, and hidden pain. The specific patterns and tendencies of the subtypes vary depending on which of the three survival instincts dominates your experience.

Self-Preservation 3 Subtype

This subtype wants to *be* good, not just *look* good. They focus on providing good models for whatever role they play, as determined by social consensus. They can be the most extreme workaholics of all twenty-seven personalities. Their survival strategies, along with a self-preservation instinct that fuels anxiety about material security, make them work really hard. They want to present a good image, but their need to be good means they don't want to be seen as excessively self-promoting or to brag about their achievements. They are more modest, less vain, and not as competitive as the Social 3 subtype.

Social 3 Subtype

This subtype likes to be on stage more than the other two and enjoys recognition and applause the most. They are the most skilled at crafting a flawless image and know how to package and market whatever they are selling (including themselves). This subtype finds comfort in leadership positions and shows great skill at climbing the corporate or social ladder. This is the most aggressive and competitive subtype. They want to win and know how to influence others through an effective presentation or performance.

Sexual (One-to-One) 3 Subtype

This subtype focuses the most on one-to-one relationships—and on being attractive as defined by conventional standards. They may see attracting a partner in highly romanticized, fairy-tale terms. They know how to be charismatic and appealing, but focus on their outer presentation and may be disconnected from their inner experience of who they really are. They are more emotional than the other subtypes and often feel a sense of sadness deep inside. They put a lot of attention on supporting others and helping them succeed. They are more shy than the other subtypes and not as competitive, because they succeed when the people they support succeed.

The Type 3 Subtype Shadows

You can more effectively confront your own Shadow if you know the specific shadow characteristics of your Type 3 subtype. Below are some of the shadow aspects of each subtype. As subtype behavior can be highly automatic, these traits can be hardest to see and own.

Self-Preservation 3 Shadow

If this is your subtype, you may have a difficult (or impossible) time slowing down. Your anxiety about survival and being good means that your ego tells you that you can't stop working. You are likely overly autonomous and self-sufficient and may find it hard to depend on or connect with others. You not only strive endlessly to look good, you also want to do things right. Unlike Type 1s, however, you determine what's "right" by looking outside yourself. You probably have great difficulty feeling deeper emotions and expressing vulnerability. You can be excessively modest and get trapped in a vicious cycle of wanting to *look* good, wanting to *be* good, and wanting to *do* good. But you may not be able to relax and feel successful in any of this.

Social 3 Shadow

If this is your subtype, you are likely good at creating a really great image, but tend to become attached to always having a flawless image. You may feel vulnerable if people see beyond the image you present to the world. You may not even allow yourself to be fully aware of the true self that lies behind your persona. Your strong need to compete and win can make you ruthless—you may do anything to come out on top. You may try to lie, cheat, or steal to win, all while hiding these behaviors behind a positive image. You likely have great difficulty with failure and may do whatever you can to avoid it, especially if you feel insecure. You need the applause of the crowd to feel worthy and may avoid developing real inner security to the extent that you hide behind a superficially successful image.

Sexual (One-to-One) 3 Shadow

If this is your subtype, you focus much of your attention on others. Your need to be attractive on the outside means you often lose contact with who you really are on the inside. You likely feel a deep sense of sadness about not being in touch with yourself and you may tend to have low self-esteem. You probably have a difficult time accessing this sadness, however, even though it can help connect you with your authentic self. You support others and achieve success through working to help them achieve their accomplishments as a way to avoid being seen.

> "What brings order in the world is to love and let love do what it will." —Krishnamurti

The Type 3 Paradox

The Type 3 paradox is grounded in the polarity between the passion of self-deceit and the virtue of veracity. By recognizing the need they have to be viewed positively at all costs and to earn the admiration of others, this type begins to see their self-deceit in action. If you identify with this type, you must examine all the ways you deceive yourself. By learning to tell the difference between your false self (your ideal image) and your true self, you move from the conviction that you are what you do, to realizing *from the inside* who you truly are. As you become aware of your own self-deceit, you begin to know and state what you really want and how you really feel—first to yourself and then to others.

In this context, veracity means accessing a deeper truth—the inherent truthfulness inside yourself and the heart's unwillingness to be what you are not. Becoming aware of this paradox and learning to see how they deceive themselves into thinking they *are* their image constitute one of the main goals of the Type 3 growth journey.

If you identify with this type, here are some things you can do to become more conscious of self-deceit and more able to access the higher-level experience that veracity makes possible:

- Notice the difference between your image and what you really think and feel.

- Acknowledge all the different personae you adopt in the different areas of your life. Are you someone different at work and at home? Are you different during the week and on weekends? Do you present a different image to one particular group of friends as opposed to another? If so, why?

- Examine your tendency to maintain a fast pace of activity in your life. Ask yourself if one reason you do so much without stopping is that you are running away from your emotions.

- Recognize how little space you leave for your feelings. Consider that, in your case and at this point, your feelings are one of the clearest indicators of your true self. Allow yourself to feel your emotions, little by little, as a way of getting to know more of the truth of who you are.

- Become aware of what keeps you from slowing down. Notice any fear or anxiety you may feel that may be connected to acknowledging your feelings and questioning your identity.

- Notice all the little ways you lie to yourself and others about who you are. Question and explore the ways you deceive yourself.

· ·

"Avoidance of self-deception is a matter of integrity
not comfort." —Orrin Woodward

· ·

Using Type 3 Arrow Lines for Growth

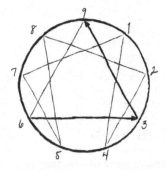

The two personality types connected to Type 3 by the internal lines within the Enneagram diagram are Types 6 and 9. This type can create a big shift from their usual focus on tasks, achieving goals, and gaining recognition by embodying Type 6 tendencies to slow down, access concerns, and assess threats. They can then learn to be more available for connection with people by integrating Type 9 insights. These insights also help them develop their capacity to relax and connect more deeply with others.

- First, develop Type 6's ability to explore potential problems that may arise as you consider a task or goal. Pause to think about what could go wrong and consider possible threats and risks before getting started on plans and projects. Question what's happening before you jump to your next task. Get in touch with any fears and anxieties you may have about what you are doing and give yourself time to explore those concerns as a way of deepening your thinking about work and relationships. Engage in healthy self-doubt as a way to get in touch with your true feelings and your real self.

- Then integrate Type 9 strengths by slowing down even more and focusing on becoming more receptive and humble. Broaden your focus from the shortest path to the goal and getting timely results, to what's good for others. Listen more fully to others and consider their views when delivering on goals. Develop the ability to follow others' agendas instead of always leading the charge to deliver on your own. Balance your work focus with more attention to creating connection and harmony in your relationships and with yourself. Live a more balanced life and do more activities that relax you.

> "Perhaps the greatest self-deceit is to tell ourselves that we can be self-sufficient." —Joseph Stowell

EMBRACING THE HIGH SIDE

On the third part of their journey, this type embraces more of who they really are *beyond* the images they create and the roles they play. They reduce the energy they spend crafting a specific image and sink more deeply into a genuine connection with their emotions and their true selves. When they consciously work to become more self-aware, integrate their blind spots, and access their pain, they learn to know and appreciate themselves at a much deeper level—in a way they may never have thought possible.

When Type 3s do this work, they get to know their inner truth beyond their egoic need for positive feedback and admiration. When they realize that they don't need to put on masks to be worthy of love and respect, they begin to live from a remembrance of their true selves and stop thinking that they have to be the one who keeps the whole world spinning. They discover that they don't need to be anything other than who they are to have value and achieve positive outcomes.

The higher state of consciousness this type can attain is characterized by love, unity, and connection with others and the universe. In this state, working so hard to be accepted or central to what's happening makes no sense. The belief that they need to have a specific title or achievement or image to be important and valuable has no meaning.

If you identify with this type, here are some things you can work on to continue to make progress at this third stage of your growth journey:

- Recognize that you are not your personality so you can contact your real self—your true identity. Let your "inner observer" clearly see that, when you live through your persona, that is not "who you are." You can tell the difference between your false self and your true self.

- Stay in touch with your heart; be beautifully emotional without apology or embarrassment. Notice how this impacts others positively and how nice it feels when you allow your emotional state to produce results without doing anything.

- Enjoy the experience of just being. Own how good it feels to live in an essential state of truthfulness.

- Value your inner sense of worth over your need for praise or recognition from the outside.

- Identify what you truly want and like. Notice how good it feels to make choices based on your natural desires rather than on what others value.

- Collaborate closely with others in your life and your work. Listen deeply to their thoughts and feelings to inform the things you do.

- Build stronger relationships by being more authentic and more known by others. Allow yourself to depend on others to do things for you.

- Learn how much you actually need to do and how central you actually need to be for things to happen. Allow for your activity to be more limited. Do only what is necessary for you to do.

- Win people over through the authentic expression of how you feel and what you want.

"Love takes off the masks we fear we cannot live without and know we cannot live within." —James Baldwin

The Type 3 Virtue

Veracity is the virtue that provides an antidote to the Type 3 passion of self-deceit. For this type, veracity involves being more fully conscious of the deception implicit in their personality structure. It means recognizing their false selves as false and learning not to find their identity in what others want them to be or how they would like to appear to others.

Veracity requires radical transparency and a clearly felt sense of being grounded in your inner being. It means listening to your heart to discover the difference between the truth and the lie within you. It generates a good feeling about the real you and an appreciation of the fullness and satisfaction of living from the truth of who you are. It means knowing and expressing the truth with everyone you encounter every day, and being more at ease and relaxed in life as you experience the natural flow arising from your true being.

If you identify with this type, veracity will allow you to see the ultimate value in living your truth and simply *being*. In fact, veracity is not only a willingness of the heart to be just who you *are*; it is also an unwillingness of the heart to be who you are *not*. By consciously studying all the ways you have lied to yourself as part of your survival strategy, you learn the difference between the true and the false, and stop adapting and shape-shifting. You discover your authentic self and become intolerant of anything fake in yourself or in others.

As a Type 3 in the state of veracity, you start to experience:

- A life grounded in the knowledge of the truth of who and what you are, informed by your deepest nature.

- Acceptance of people who don't like or value you, because you have no need to impress them or gain their approval.

- Recognition of your heart's capacity to touch and influence people emotionally.

- A state of being in which your expressions, interactions, and activities display the deepest truth of how you feel, what you value, and what you want.

- An ability to question and explore all the ways in which you deceive yourself and a capacity to forgive yourself when you inadvertently get enmeshed in the illusions of conventional reality.

- A sense of being present to the truth of what is happening inside you in the moment, rather than in reference to what may be happening on the outside.

- An ongoing connection to your depths more than to superficial reality and the needs of the ego, which allows you to more deeply and authentically connect with others.

. . . .

"You can't know your real mind as long as
you deceive yourself." —Bodidharma

. . . .

Waking Up from the Zombie State

For Type 3, the key to embracing their true selves lies in gradually learning to know and like their authentic selves more than their egoic selves. This happens as they strengthen their sense of who they are without needing to take on a specific role or persona. When they become conscious of their tendency to deceive themselves and learn to catch themselves in the act of shape-shifting, they learn that their true selves can be available for love and connection while their false selves cannot.

When they reach this third stage of their journey, this type shifts from having a mostly outward focus to being able to pay more attention to what's going on inside. They cultivate a new ability to access the truth of who they are and what they want. They become conscious of the ways they alter their persona to appeal to others as a way of earning love and appreciation, and they learn that they can really be loved only when they stop trying to prove that they are competent or productive. They release the need to be high achievers and relax into a more confident sense of who they are from the inside.

This pathway can be challenging because of the way Type 3 survival strategies get reinforced and rewarded in many cultures. It can be hard to see the need for change if your personality style works so well to attain the things that society recognizes as markers of a good or a successful person. Moreover, this type may have difficulty separating their real identity from their personality patterns and distinguishing the false from the true because of their specific defense mechanisms. But this is something they must do to wake up from the zombie state they live in when ruled by their egos. They must understand that they are much more than their personality, because unless they do, they limit their ability to live a more conscious life and grow to their full potential.

When Type 3s take the journey of self-development, however, and wake up to the fact that they are not just what they do or how they look, they can bring the richness of who they are to the world in ways they can't even imagine. They realize that true success lies in their ability to know who they truly are and begin to live from a grounded sense of being in touch with their depths. And when they do this, they not only open the door to truly loving themselves, they make themselves available to be deeply loved by others for who they really are.

We end this chapter with this quote from the classic story, *The Velveteen Rabbit*, by Margery Williams. It perfectly sums up what it means for Type 3s to love themselves and let others love them—through coming to know their essential realness.

> "What is real?" asked the Rabbit one day, when they were lying side by side near the nursery fender, before Nans came to tidy the room. "Does it mean having things that buzz inside you and a stick-out handle?"

"Real isn't how you are made," said the Skin Horse. "It's a thing that happens to you. When a child loves you for a long, long time, not just to play with, but really loves you, then you become Real."

"Does it hurt?" asked the Rabbit.

"Sometimes," said the Skin Horse, for he was always truthful. "When you are Real, you don't mind being hurt."

"Does it happen all at once, like being wound up," he asked, "or bit by bit?"

"It doesn't happen all at once," said the Skin Horse. "You become. It takes a long time. That's why it doesn't happen often to people who break easily, or have sharp edges, or who have to be carefully kept. Generally, by the time you are Real, most of your hair has been loved off, and your eyes drop out and you get loose in the joints and very shabby. But these things don't matter at all, because once you are Real you can't be ugly, except to people who don't understand."

Weeks passed, and the little Rabbit grew very old and shabby, but the Boy loved him just as much. He loved him so hard that he loved all his whiskers off, and the pink lining to his ears turned grey, and his brown spots faded. He even began to lose his shape, and he scarcely looked like a rabbit anymore, except to the Boy. To him he was always beautiful, and that was all that the little Rabbit cared about. He didn't mind how he looked to other people, because the nursery magic had made him Real, and when you are Real, shabbiness doesn't matter.

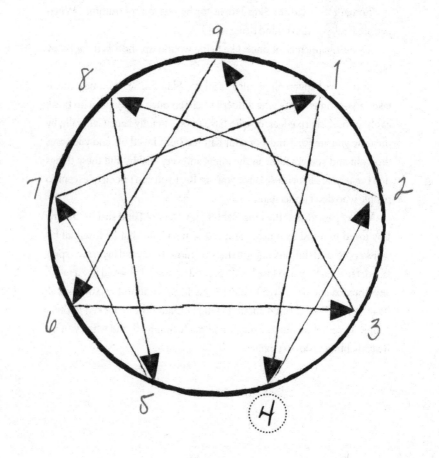

The Path from Envy to Equanimity

Envy is the art of counting the other fellow's blessings instead of your own.

HAROLD COFFIN

Gratitude, not understanding, is the secret to joy and equanimity.

ANNE LAMOTT

O nce upon a time, there was a person named Four. When she was young, she thought she had a total connection to the world—with nature and the people around her. She felt cherished by her parents, as all children should. But then something happened that changed everything. A baby was born. It was as if Four's perfect world ended. No longer was she the center of her parents' attention. No longer was she the most special child in the world. When she wanted someone to play with or a hug, everyone was busy taking care of the baby. She felt unimportant, alone, and ordinary.

Four made sense of this terrible new situation by believing that she must have done something wrong to cause the loss of connection with her parents. After all, they didn't seem to care about her the way they did before. It must have been her fault. They must have discovered there was something wrong with her. This new baby must somehow be better. What other explanation could there be?

Four's new way of thinking caused her some pain and distress, but gradually she got used to feeling bad—and sad. And, she reasoned, if it was her fault that she had lost the connection she had once felt—maybe that meant she could do something to make things right. Maybe she could somehow make a connection with others and the world again by showing everyone how special she was— or by making them see how much she was suffering by acknowledging that she wasn't as special as she had thought. In the meantime, her sadness became a familiar friend that kept her company when she was lonely.

Over time, Four tried different ways to rebuild the connection she had lost. She tried to get people to see her as special again. She showed them how extraordinary and unique she was by drawing beautiful pictures, saying authentic things, and expressing her emotional depth by singing sad songs. But no one seemed to notice her specialness. They just said she was being "too sensitive" or "too dramatic." She tried telling people all the intricate details of her pain and loss, in hopes that they would do something to ease her suffering. She tried to show how strong she was by withstanding her suffering without complaining. She tried getting angry and competing with others to prove her superiority. But no one ever gave her the understanding and deep connection she longed for.

None of her efforts made Four feel understood or special, but eventually these ways of feeling, thinking, and acting became habits. She couldn't stop longing for love, understanding, and deep connection, but she also couldn't stop believing that she was totally unworthy of those things. Driven by the need to feel connected again, she continued to focus on and experience the emotions she felt about the love she had lost. She couldn't stop seeing all her flaws. She couldn't stop noticing all the good things that others had that were missing in her life— and yearning for someone or something to help her feel worthy.

Without realizing it, the strategies Four had adopted to cope with her feeling of loss came to rule her life. A lot of people thought it odd that she tried to get love and understanding by focusing on being unworthy of it. But every once in a while, her strategy did work to get her some attention, even if it was negative attention. And that just reinforced her habits.

Occasionally, someone *would* see that Four was special and try to give her the love she longed for. But by that time, she was totally convinced that she didn't deserve love because she hadn't been good enough to keep it early on. And she couldn't receive love when it was offered. She couldn't stop creating situations that confirmed her belief in her own inadequacy. She couldn't stop pushing people away to make sure that they couldn't abandon her. Because she knew they would. She would always be disappointed. Trying to believe anything else only increased her pain. It was better to be sad all the time to protect herself from the hope of something good—something that she couldn't allow to happen anyway.

Four had become a zombie—a very authentic, emotional zombie, but a zombie just the same.

THE TYPE 4 CHECKLIST

If most or all of the following personality traits apply to you, you may be a Type 4:

- ☑ You focus much of your attention on the inner workings of your emotions. You experience a wide range of emotions, and you are comfortable with intense feelings.

- ☑ You can easily see what's missing in any situation—and in yourself.

- ☑ You often compare yourself to others—sometimes favorably, sometimes unfavorably.

- ☑ You feel that you don't fit in—in both good and bad ways.

- ☑ You are familiar with the experience of sadness.

- ☑ You easily feel what's going on at a deeper level when people interact—what's going on beneath the surface that's not being expressed.

- ☑ You place a high value on authenticity—in yourself and others. When you feel the need to tell the truth, people sometimes appreciate it and sometimes they don't.

- ☑ You easily tune in to how connected or disconnected you are from someone else; you are sensitive to the space between yourself and others.

- ☑ You have a strong desire to feel understood, although you often feel misunderstood.

If, after using this checklist, you find that you are a Type 4, your growth journey will follow three steps.

First, you will embark on a quest to know yourself more deeply by identifying personality patterns that lead you to limit yourself by focusing on what's missing and not ideal, and on all the ways you feel inadequate or different.

Then you must face your Shadow to learn how you actually create more misunderstanding and disconnection by dwelling on an inner experience of lack—and how seeing yourself as inadequate means you disown your strengths and gifts. By courageously examining these ego patterns, you begin to understand how they are blocking your growth.

The final stage of your journey involves letting go of your false self and owning more of your true—or higher—self to become more whole. When you do this, you become more open to real connection with yourself and others by rising above your emotional ups and downs and recognizing what is positive in you and already present in your life.

. . . .

"Folks are usually about as happy as they make their minds
up to be." —Abraham Lincoln

. . . .

EMBARKING ON THE QUEST

The first stage of the Type 4 growth journey involves consciously observing their mental pattern of comparing themselves to others. When they start to see all the ways in which they confirm their belief in their own deficiency and begin to acknowledge those habits as a defense against discovering they are as good as anyone else, they initiate their journey to knowing and accepting all of who they truly are.

If you identify as a Type 4, your journey starts with recognizing (without judging) how much attention you give to your internal fantasies and how little attention you give to the reality of who you are and how you are actually received by others. Once you become aware of how you create negative scenarios in your life by holding negative beliefs about yourself that aren't really true, you have taken the first step on your path.

Key Type 4 Patterns

Most Type 4s think that acknowledging their inadequacy somehow makes them honest or authentic. In reality, however, this only cements a defensive pattern in which everything they experience gets interpreted as affirming their sense of lack. Because they can't see and interrupt this false belief in their own deficiency—and notice the way it operates as a defense to keep them from opening up to good things—they stay asleep and fail to grow. But to make progress on their journey, they need to see that looking for evidence of their own inferiority or superiority (which also reflects a deeper sense of inferiority) keeps them stuck in an illusion about who they are, and this blocks them from manifesting all they are capable of being. Waking up for this type means questioning their belief that they aren't enough. It also means recognizing that they have created an identity out of being unworthy.

If you identify with this type, your journey begins with focusing on and making more conscious these five habitual Type 4 patterns.

Devaluing the Present

Notice if you tend to idealize what's distant and see only what's lacking in the present. Observe yourself to see if you glorify or regret the past and fantasize about the future. Check to see if your mind moves away from enjoying and embracing what's happening *now* by continually contemplating missed opportunities or a rosy picture of what could happen in a more satisfying future. You may often think in terms of "the grass being greener" somewhere else and this takes you away from the only time in which you can actually take action—the present moment. This may tend to create a push-pull dynamic in your relationships that makes others seem more attractive when they are unavailable to you.

Comparing Yourself to Others

When you observe yourself, you may notice you have a "comparing mind." Check to see if you automatically compare yourself to what you perceive in others. This means you likely regularly contrast elements of yourself with what others have or do and usually come out on the bottom. But whether you feel inferior or superior, in your mind you are never equal—someone is always better or worse than you are. You may tend to put a lot of focus on assessing people and feeling bad about being "less than" others. You probably often feel that others have good qualities that are missing in you. Or, at times, you may get competitive and see yourself as better than others.

Living Mostly in Your Inner World

Notice if you tend to focus your attention on what's happening inside you—on your feelings, thoughts, and fantasies. This causes you to develop a biased perception of who you are, despite the fact that you may think you are being objective about your limitations. Much of the time, you may resist taking in positive feedback from others and feel certain you are right in your self-assessments. By living inside yourself so much, you prevent yourself from taking in the reality outside you and being present with what's actually happening. You will need to observe yourself to see if you actually live a life based on false impressions about yourself in a way that holds you back. It will be important to consider that, when you focus so much on your inner feelings and stories about yourself, you block yourself from acknowledging the possibility of being more fulfilled by being in touch with (good) things as they actually are.

Assuming Your Emotions Define You

You likely rely too much on your own emotions to define your experience of the world, thus skewing your perception of what's really happening and potentially contributing to others' perceptions that you are overly sensitive or self-absorbed. Descartes famously said: "I think therefore I am." But you may live by, and never question, a similar idea: "I feel therefore I am." Notice if you equate all of your experience of life to what you are feeling emotionally, and check to see if this can function as a self-limiting habit. Your emotions are important, of course, but they come and go—they aren't all of who you are. They bring information and wisdom about what's important to you—but they are meant to be felt, processed, and then let go.

Believing in Your Own Unworthiness

You may often judge yourself to be either lacking or superior, but believe, deeper down, that you are deficient in some fundamental way. And you may continually make comparisons to confirm a sense of your own inadequacy. Check to see if you tend to convince yourself that you lack some needed qualities that would make you whole or worthy or lovable, and if you tend to assume that you are not good enough. Notice if you allow your thoughts and feelings to reinforce this (false) belief, and ask yourself if this stops you from owning who you really are.

> "When one door of happiness closes, another opens; but often we look so long at the closed door that we do not see the one which has opened for us." —Helen Keller

The Type 4 Passion

Envy is the passion that drives the Type 4 personality. In its expression as this passion, envy is the desire to have for yourself positive aspects that someone else has. The Latin root of the word "envy" is *invidere*, meaning "to look upon." In the Purgatory section of Dante's *Divine Comedy*, he portrays the souls who "purge" the passion of envy as having their eyes sewn shut with wire so that they can't see what others have that they want. Envy includes a painful sense of missing something essential, as well as a craving for that which is felt to be lacking. This type is always aware of how they don't measure up to an ideal of what they should be—and how others do fit this ideal in ways they do not.

Envy operates to keep this type focused on what they don't have. It contributes to an inner sense that they are not whole and sufficient as they are. Their envy can be destructive in its effects by encouraging resentment of others whom they perceive as more whole or worthy than they are, not realizing that this may be a projection of their own disowned positive qualities. In other words, they attribute positive qualities to others without realizing that they are placing their own goodness outside themselves. At the same time, envy makes this type close their hearts to themselves and to the people they envy, effectively blocking them from owning or taking in the goodness for which they long.

If you identify with this type, here are some typical manifestations of envy you must observe and make more conscious if you want to move forward on your path to awakening:

- Focusing more on what's missing than on what's present.

- Focusing on positive attributes you lack and feeling intensely self-critical. Comparing what others have to what you have, and always feeling worse off or better off, but never equal.

- Praising or admiring others excessively or giving enthusiastic compliments.

- Disdaining others or being harshly critical of them.

- Having or perpetuating a superiority or inferiority complex. Looking up to others or down on them.

- Being overly excited or overly sad about situations.

- Feeling competitive and acting in ways motivated by overt or covert competition.

- Self-referencing and focusing primarily on your own experience and how things relate to you.

- Needing to feel special; promoting high standards and never being satisfied or content.

· ·
"He who envies others does not obtain peace of mind."
—Buddha
· ·

Using Type 4 Wings as Growth Stretches

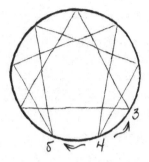

The two personality types adjacent to Type 4 on the Enneagram circle are Types 3 and 5. Type 3 qualities help 4s become more pragmatic and less emotional, while Type 5 qualities help them become more objective and balanced. This broadens their habitual focus on connections, emotions, and relationships, and allows them to develop their capacity to be more practical in different ways.

- First, embody Type 3's ability to prioritize tasks over feelings and work to become more efficient and pragmatic. Focus on work, goals, and practical tasks to divert attention from the emotions you dwell on more than you need to. Let go of whatever feelings threaten to distract you from what needs to be done. Get interested in the positive emotions that come with the accomplishment of successful work outcomes. When you notice yourself amping up intense emotions, try dialing down the emotional volume and increasing your focus on your "to do" list.

- Then integrate Type 5 traits by noticing when you feel overwhelmed by a strong emotion and making a conscious effort to be more calm and balanced. Analyze your feelings to "make sense of" whatever is happening. Learn to recognize when you focus too intently on emotions and shift your attention from your feelings to your thoughts. Learn to extract information from your emotions about what is important to you and then detach from them in a healthy way. Practice moving from your heart to your head to become more objective about what's happening and put your feelings in a larger context. Balance your focus on relating to people with choosing to disengage and enjoy time alone.

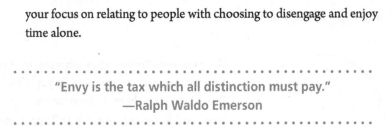

"Envy is the tax which all distinction must pay."
—Ralph Waldo Emerson

FACING THE SHADOW

The second part of the growth journey for this type involves recognizing how they try to be understood and appreciated by over-focusing on their suffering as a way to earn love, and acknowledging, owning, and integrating all the positive aspects of their life experience. When they do this, they learn to identify less with what they perceive as a deficient self and focus more on simplicity, gratitude, and contentedness.

On this part of their journey, this type begins to realize that their focus on their inner emotional truth (which they thought was a good thing) can be a bad thing. Their lack of self-awareness can make them melodramatic or masochistic, self-absorbed, and demanding, even while they consciously think that they are exquisitely sensitive, empathic, and honest. When they are overly focused on their inner territory and dwell too much in melancholy, they can become self-centered, emotionally overwhelmed, excessively negative, and overly committed to making others see them as extraordinary. When others don't mirror back their desire to be seen as unique, they can become withdrawn, moody, or openly angry. They may focus on their "negatives" and not see what's positive. This part of their path can be embarrassing and hard to own without getting caught up in feeling even worse about themselves. The key for them is not to judge themselves, and to know that owning their Shadow means seeing the truth of their worthiness and learning to feel better about themselves.

Meeting the Type 4 Shadow

If you identify as a Type 4, here are some actions you can take to bring to the surface, become more aware of, and start counteracting the key unconscious patterns, blind spots, and pain points of this type:

- Balance respect for your feelings with an ability to let go of emotions after you have felt, processed, and shared them.

- Get more grounded in your body so you can be more practical and focused on what you need to do right now.

- Move on from specific emotions by consciously shifting from feelings to mental analysis.

- Develop your capacity to be present in the here and now. If you get pulled into nostalgia for the past or idealistic yearning for the future, consciously refocus on "what is" right now.

- Balance your focus on what's going on inside you with an awareness of other people's feelings, needs, and desires.

- Notice, explore, and work against your tendency to "introject" (or take in) other people's emotional states as an unconscious way to control what's happening in key relationships.

- When you realize you have unconsciously taken on something from someone else that is not yours, give it back to them.

- Become aware of the ways in which you devalue yourself and avoid owning the good in yourself. Nourish yourself by actively taking in what's positive.

- Practice putting your attention and energy outside yourself to balance your internal, self-referencing focus.

> "I thought the most beautiful thing in the world
> must be shadow." —Sylvia Plath

The Type 4 Blind Spots

This type may not want to examine their blind spots because they tend to get attached to specific emotional states. Unlike others, who avoid blind spots to stay happy, they may avoid happiness in order to experience some sort of satisfaction in feeling bad—or sad or mad. They may genuinely feel insecure, but their specific zombie survival strategies amplify their feelings of discontent as a defense against an even deeper pain.

This type resists looking inward at the good stuff they don't see in themselves—and don't see they don't see—because they get comfortable with disappointment or discontent. They don't want to risk feeling better for fear that they will be abandoned again or fail in some way. But getting stuck in a negative mood that shields them from feeling worse just blocks their growth. When they get attached to feeling bad, they don't allow themselves to see that their negative self-image is distorted. They actually have many reasons to feel good about themselves—but this is what gets hidden in their blind spots.

If you identify with this type, the good news is that, if you are willing to look at your blind spots and open up to having good feelings about yourself, you can live from a truly authentic sense of your best self in a way you didn't think possible. If you can endure the shock and dismay of learning you are actually happy (!) and see this as good news, you can learn to feel glad about who you are.

Here are some of the central blind spots you must make more conscious as a Type 4 to move forward on your journey.

Not Seeing What's Good

Do you see only what's wrong in you and your life and not what's great? Do you tend to focus on what's lacking in yourself or your present situation instead of on all that is good and working well? Here are some things you can do to integrate this blind spot:

- Make a list of all your positive attributes. Question your sense of what's negative in you and keep adding to the list of your positive qualities.

- Ask your closest friends and family members to tell you all the things they love about you. Write them down and look at this list every day. Breathe in your goodness. Take it in completely.

- Practice being in the present moment without thinking about the past or the future. Notice what's good right now.

- Observe any positive things you notice about the people around you. Consider whether any of these are projections of what is good in you—traits you attribute to others that are actually yours.

- Notice the reality of what many spiritual teachings tell us—that we all have equal value. Remind yourself repeatedly that no one is better or worse than anyone else. All comparisons to the contrary are misperceptions.

- Work to integrate the good aspects of yourself that you deny. Do "mirror work"; practice saying positive affirmations to yourself in front of a mirror and let them land inside you.

Over-Identifying with Emotions

Do you believe you *are* your feelings? Do you focus on ideals and perceptions that take too much of their meaning from your inner state and not from the rest of reality? Try some of these techniques to help integrate this blind spot:

- Be more aware of any beliefs you hold that your whole identity is mainly about your emotions or your capacity for emotional depth.

- When you believe something based solely on an emotion, do a "reality check" by mentally consulting the evidence of what is really happening outside you. Do this several times a day.

- Practice shifting your attention from how you feel to what is really happening in the world around you.

- Become aware of how you live for long periods of time within yourself—within your rich emotional or fantasy life.

- Regularly shift your focus from your internal state to what's happening with the people around you—to really finding out what they are thinking, feeling, and experiencing.

- Ask the people with whom you interact more about themselves and tell them less about you. Listen fully to them without internalizing what they share—i.e., put yourself in their shoes.

Seeking Understanding in Ways That Prevent It

Do you assume everyone experiences emotions the same way you do? Do you devalue people who undervalue (or avoid feeling) emotions. Do you avoid taking responsibility when misunderstandings persist in your relationships? Here are some things you can do to integrate this blind spot:

- Notice and own how important being fully understood by others is to you and explore what this means for you.

- Observe the ways you try to make yourself understood by the people in your life and check in with others to see if they work.

- Become more aware of the ways you communicate your emotions to people who do not relate to emotions in the same way you do. Realize that you may need to educate people about how emotional you are and how much you need to feel understood.

- Explore your tendency to amp up your emotions (or your emotional intensity) in response to feeling misunderstood.

- Avoid using language that is too sophisticated or abstract (or metaphoric), as it may prevent others from understanding you. Learn how to communicate more directly and simply.

- Practice balancing emotions and mental activity when communicating with others—especially people who experience discomfort in the face of emotions.

"Envy is a symptom of lack of appreciation of our own uniqueness and self-worth." —Elizabeth O'Connor

Type 4 Pain

Type 4s have a hard time recognizing, fully integrating, and moving on from their pain. It may seem that they don't need to "feel their pain" because they are usually already experiencing quite a lot of it. They also tend to be strong and resilient in the face of pain because they feel more comfortable with difficult emotions than the other types. But this type needs to experience specific kinds of pain more consciously and confront other emotions that they unconsciously avoid as part of their survival strategy. This can be tricky for them, because they tend to focus too much on some forms of suffering and are sometimes even stereotyped as suffering too much. But while it's true that this type can overdo its tendency to suffer, that's not the whole picture.

The journey of awakening is about consciously suffering the particular pain your Enneagram type needs to address to grow. If you identify as a Type 4, the suffering you express when acting from your false self is a kind of unconscious, mechanical repetition of the same painful themes that may seem like the pain you need to feel to integrate your Shadow, but it's not. You may dwell too much in melancholy, sadness, hopelessness, and different kinds of pain as part of your survival strategy. To become more whole through the growth process, however, you must learn to see the difference between wallowing in pain as a defense mechanism and facing the pain you avoid.

Type 4s must become more aware of how they over-indulge in sadness and other emotions as a defense against consciously experiencing happy feelings, fear of abandonment, and the pain and grief connected with loss and abandonment. The deeper pain they avoid the most is the pain that reminds them of the loss of connection they experienced early on. They fear re-experiencing that loss more than anything else. This is why it may be hard for them to feel good about themselves. Being happy creates the possibility of being surprised by being abandoned all over again. Once they allow themselves to hope that they are worthy of love, the specter of abandonment, grief, and disappointment raises its ugly head. Ironically, feeling good about themselves can feel like setting themselves up for a fall. And preventing these feelings by proactively pushing people away can be a powerful way to avoid the pain of being left again.

It can be difficult for this type to confront specific feelings connected to the reality that they actually may be worthy and whole. It may be hard for them to open up to the possibility of being loved for who they are. It may be easier to hide out in sadness as a defense against feeling good—since feeling good (loved) means they have something to lose (again).

If you identify as a Type 4, you must learn to tolerate these specific painful feelings to move forward on your growth journey:

- Fear of abandonment. Fear of trying and failing to forge authentic, satisfying connections and being disappointed. Fear of hoping you will be understood and appreciated and then learning it's not possible because something really is wrong with you. Fear of having your worst fears realized about your lack of worth.

- Shame connected to being seen, exposed, and potentially abandoned. Shame connected to your (false) belief in your own ultimate deficiency. Shame that operates as part of the false self when it shuts down your access to deeper pain—and the possibility of relief from that pain—that needs to be accessed.

- Grief related to an early experience of loss of connection. Grief that pulls you in and makes you take refuge in superficial versions of this important emotion. Grief at not being loved as you should have been or wanted to be, or for all you lost when you felt abandoned. You need to access your deepest layer of grief at disconnection—from the original love object or from "origin" or "source" itself. And then you need to let it go.

- Pain connected to being misunderstood, rejected, or abandoned by important people in your life. You need to access the deepest levels of this pain, as you may defend against it by feeling a shallower version of hopelessness or melancholy.

- Anger that you repress or feel guilty about—or act out in unhealthy ways. Anger helps you stand up for yourself and take ownership of positive qualities. Depending on your subtype, you may dwell too much in anger to defend against pain; you need to feel the pain under the anger.

- Happiness and joy that you avoid feeling when you focus too much on sadness, grief, fear, or shame. You need to feel, own, and embrace the experience of being truly happy, without searching for what may be missing.

"The worst part of success is trying to find someone who is happy for you." —Bette Midler

The Type 4 Subtypes

Identifying your Type 4 subtype can help you more precisely target your efforts to confront your blind spots, unconscious tendencies, and hidden pain. The specific patterns and tendencies of the subtypes vary depending on which of the three survival instincts dominates your experience.

Self-Preservation 4 Subtype

This subtype internalizes suffering and feels emotions inside, but doesn't share them with others. They are stoic and strong in the face of difficult feelings, and sometimes in response to a belief that, to be "loved," they have to be tough or happy or endure pain alone. They are hardworking and action-oriented. They don't always feel envy consciously, but instead work to prove themselves worthy. They tend to be more masochistic than melodramatic, and may look happy or "okay" on the outside while struggling to endure hardship on the inside without showing it. They are self-sufficient and autonomous, and try to heal the pain of the world, even if that entails exerting a lot of effort.

Social 4 Subtype

This subtype dwells more in suffering and communicates more about their painful emotions. They may tend to be overly sensitive and often appear sad. They express sensitivity, melancholy, and unhappiness more readily than the other Type 4 subtypes. They frequently compare themselves to others and then focus a great deal of attention on the emotional suffering they feel at seeing themselves as inferior to or less worthy than others. They remain convinced there's something wrong with them, even in the face of evidence to the contrary.

Sexual (One-to-One) 4 Subtype

This subtype externalizes suffering. They are often called the "mad 4" because they express anger easily, usually in response to feeling misunderstood or deprived. They focus on communicating anger to defend against pain, shame, or feelings of deficiency. This is the most competitive Type 4 subtype. Their envy manifests as competition and drives active efforts to be affirmed as special and superior. They want to be seen as attractive, special, or extraordinary compared to others. They may have a tendency toward arrogance.

The Type 4 Subtype Shadows

You can more effectively confront your own Shadow if you know the specific shadow characteristics of your Type 4 personality subtype. Below are some of the shadow characteristics of each subtype. As subtype behavior can be highly automatic, these traits can be the hardest to see and own.

Self-Preservation 4 Shadow

If this is your subtype, you tend toward masochism, not realizing that you are excessively hard on yourself and never allow for lightness or fragility. You dislike being identified as a victim, and you likely received messages in childhood that people didn't want to hear about your pain, so you feel you need to prove your worth by suffering silently and enduring hardship and pain without showing or sharing it. You may put on a happy face, even when you feel deeply sad or stressed inside. You have a tendency to carry a lot of pain without being aware of it—both psychological and physical. You must learn to share your pain with others and allow yourself to be supported.

Social 4 Shadow

If this is your subtype, you become overly attached to feeling and expressing suffering as a way to earn love. You take refuge in a victim mentality and must learn to work against this. You tend to focus too much on painful emotions, and this prevents you from taking action and being practical. You tend to be overly sensitive and attached to feelings of sadness or disappointment. You can feel guilty for feeling angry and will benefit from learning to express your anger. You need to allow for happiness in your life. Your belief in your own inferiority may actually hide a superiority complex—or a resistance to being satisfied with what's good in your life. Try to own your strengths and positive attributes.

Sexual (One-to-One) 4 Shadow

If this is your subtype, you externalize suffering to avoid feeling painful emotions and allowing yourself to be more conscious of an internal experience of sadness, hurt, or lack. You tend to focus on how others don't meet your needs as a way to avoid feeling a sense of shame and deficiency. And you may be unaware of how you express competitive tendencies as a way to "act out" your unconscious envy. It will be important to notice if you hold negative feelings toward competitors or others you view as superior to you. You can be arrogant and demanding in response to not feeling understood and not getting your needs met. To grow, you must learn to manage your anger and contact the pain under the anger.

. . . .

> "Philosophy teaches us to bear with equanimity the
> misfortunes of others." —Oscar Wilde

. . . .

The Type 4 Paradox

The Type 4 paradox arises from the polarity between the passion of envy and the virtue of equanimity. Equanimity can be understood to be a state of emotional balance that allows you to rise above the ups and downs of emotional experience and know all people and situations as having equal value. By recognizing their need to be special and unique while also feeling inferior, this type can come to understand the ways their envy operates and learn to rise above the pain of lack. As they make progress on their path to equanimity, they begin to experience a sense of inner calm, a greater capacity to modulate the ups and downs of their emotions, and an acceptance of the truth that everyone is essentially equally worthy.

If you identify as a Type 4, here are some steps you can take to become more conscious of your envy and start accessing the higher-level emotion of equanimity:

- Observe how you continually evaluate yourself relative to others. Practice shifting your attention from making comparisons to feeling grateful for what is fine in you and your life right now.

- Recognize when you feel excessively bad about yourself or excessively good about someone else. Allow yourself to appreciate that everyone is equal and let yourself feel more at ease with things as they are, instead of intensifying your feelings all the time.

- Have compassion for the part of you that thinks you are "less than" others. Let yourself feel relief at knowing that this is based on a false belief that causes you needless pain.

- Notice how you may sometimes seek to compete with or assert your superiority over others. Explore which emotions motivate this tendency and acknowledge the sense of inner peace you feel when you realize that you don't have to stand above others to feel worthy. Practice appreciating others and accessing sincere positive feelings for their good fortune without seeing this as making you inferior in any way.

- Avoid amping up the intensity of your feelings, as this takes you away from the potentially peaceful and fulfilling experience of equanimity. Notice how you may pride yourself on your intensity and ask yourself what defensive purpose this may serve.

- Notice how, without openness and an appreciation of what is good, you get caught in a vicious cycle of hungering for goodness while being unable to take it in. Observe and work against the defenses you erect against getting what you want.

"To cultivate equanimity we practice catching ourselves when we feel attraction or aversion, before it hardens into grasping or negativity." —Pema Chödrön

Using Type 4 Arrow Lines for Growth

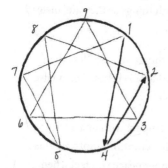

The two personality types connected to Type 4 by the lines within the Enneagram diagram are Types 1 and 2. This type can move beyond their excessive focus on their inner territory by integrating Type 1's ability to stay grounded in the body and be practical, and then developing more of Type 2's capacity to focus on and empathize deeply with others.

- First, embody the Type 1 strength of focusing on practical action steps in addition to feelings and meaning. Put your attention on what needs to be done to improve things and create high-quality results. Take action to implement your creative ideas with attention to organization, process, and discipline. Find ways to balance your emotional nature with a focus on structure and tasks. Exercise and get more in touch with your body, noticing how being more in your body helps you feel physically supported to manage fluctuating emotions.

- Then integrate Type 2's ability to balance your attention on yourself with a more intentional focus on others. Devote more attention to what others need and how you can be of service to the important people in your life. This provides a counterbalance to your self-referencing tendency and your habit of prioritizing your internal experience. Focus outside yourself; listen to others and empathize more. Strengthen your relationships through mutual understanding.

"The two virtues of equanimity and compassion become more available to the person whose ego-shell has been smashed—either by great suffering or great love—or by both." —Richard Rohr

EMBRACING THE HIGH SIDE

On the third stage of their journey, Type 4s come home to a greater realization of their true selves by relinquishing the false identity they have constructed based on their egoic need to stand out as special. This type awakens when they learn to value themselves based on their own inherent goodness—when they come to see that they don't lack anything. When they recognize they have all they need inside them, they stop imagining that something good is always out of reach or that "the grass is greener" somewhere else. When they become conscious of their envy and their need to avoid abandonment, they learn that they can be happy without sacrificing their authenticity, their emotional sensitivity, or their connection to their depths. By being grateful for all experiences in life—good and bad, light and dark—they cultivate a state of equanimity that comes from rising above the internal emotional stirrings they previously prioritized and understand that the most satisfying meaning in life comes from being present to what is happening right now.

This involves learning more about who they are beyond their egoic tendency to focus on what they don't have and how they don't measure up to a (false) ideal. They become able to shift their habit of staying preoccupied with their own flaws as a way of proving themselves. They see the downside of proactively minimizing their expectations about who they can be and what life can bring them. They realize there is nothing wrong with them and start to know that they don't always need to be understood, appreciated, and loved by others to have value. They learn that self-love is more important than being validated (or frustrated) by other people.

If you identify as a Type 4, the higher state of consciousness you can achieve at this stage of your journey is characterized by unity, equality, and a much calmer and more stable emotional atmosphere. As you rise above your need to confirm either your deficiency or your specialness, you move toward an experience of peace and generosity. You stop striving for understanding or affirmation from others and accept yourself as whole just as you are.

Here are some things you can do at this point on your journey that you couldn't have done before:

- Stop focusing on any sense of lack, understanding that lack is not inherent in you.

- See yourself as being enough and not missing anything.

- Reconnect with a deep sense of goodness.

- Welcome moments of deep calm and peace in your heart when in touch with all of yourself and everything around you.

- Allow your natural intensity to make room for balance and stability.

- Enjoy all the things that are present in your life without questioning them.

- Appreciate the absence of any need to compare yourself with others. See everyone as equally important.

- Be less emotionally sensitive without losing your emotional intelligence or your empathy for others.

- Be completely available for deep connection with others based on a humble acceptance of who you are as an ordinary happy person.

"Equanimity arises when we accept the way things are."
—Jack Kornfield

The Type 4 Virtue

Equanimity is the virtue that provides an antidote to the Type 4 passion of envy. Equanimity, understood as a state of emotional balance that allows you to rise above the ups and downs of emotional experience and see equal value in all people, feelings, and situations, helps this type grow beyond their need to feel extraordinary to have value. They stop being overly invested in any particular emotional experience, knowing that they all have equal value as reflections of their inner truth. They break away from an excessive focus on their shifting emotional states, and enjoy a remarkable sense of peace and inner calm no matter what happens or who they are with. They feel thankful for both themselves and others, knowing that everyone is equally worthy and capable of manifesting their higher potential. They acknowledge each person as unique, and that nobody is better than anybody else. They lose all their willingness to compare themselves to others and look more to reality as it is, without judging everything by their internal perceptions.

As a 4 in the state of equanimity, you start to experience:

- An appreciation of your whole self with an open mind and heart. A commitment to align with your deepest nature by being at peace and in gratitude for all you already have and all you already are.

- An ability to value all experiences as potentially meaningful—both ordinary and extraordinary—and be equally present for the whole of your life.

- A receptivity of the heart that connects you with the inherent goodness in yourself and others.

- An inner emotional balance that keeps you from being too negatively affected by external stimuli and allows you to respond to everything with exactly as much energy as is necessary.

- A state of emotional balance, even under stress, that includes a balanced view of yourself and others and is in harmony with your environment.

- A habit of accepting life on its own terms without measuring yourself against others.

- A perspective on life in its broadest sense. The ability to rise above the ebb and flow of emotions and experiences to get the highest view, where everything falls into a balanced harmony.

- A spacious stillness of mind characterized by an inner calm that allows you to be fully present through changing circumstances in life.

- A state in which you make no attempt to move away from your experience or yourself, or incorporate what looks better to you.

"Equanimity is a perfect, unshakable balance of mind."
—Nyanaponika Thera

Waking Up from the Zombie State

For Type 4s, the key to embracing their true selves lies in gradually shifting their focus from what they view as negative or missing and allowing themselves to see what's positive and present. For many people, this is difficult, as the ego tells us we are not enough, or we need to be more, or we aren't perfect enough, or we don't meet some arbitrary standard. But this type can rise above their self-defeating habit of trying to escape to an idealized past or future only by becoming conscious of their personality patterns and the ways they stay stuck in them. In fact, the only moment any of us can experience is the present. By being more present, 4s develop the ability to access their true selves and learn that all is well as it is.

When this type begins to see that they keep themselves from all they want by believing they can't have it, they open up to a larger view of who they are and enable themselves to receive in a state of gratitude. Their egoic habit of maintaining a belief in their own deficiency keeps them in zombie mode. But when they do the work they need to do to move beyond this false assumption, they achieve a state of being in which they exude inner peace and outer acceptance. They radiate joy. They appreciate all emotional experiences, but don't get thrown off balance by any of them. When they let go of their belief in their own unworthiness, they become content in the knowledge that nothing is missing. They open up to the peace, joy, and calm that are their true nature.

The Type 4 growth journey can be challenging because their belief in their inadequacy crystallizes a negative self-image at the core of the false self that becomes hard to challenge. But as this type begins to see through this lie, they recognize that their true selves are all they need—that they are adequate beyond measure. Until they work their way out of their "comparing minds," they remain trapped in a limited perspective where everything is judged in terms of better or worse. But when they learn to see beyond this narrow focus, they open up to a much more expansive—and accurate—view of themselves and others.

When Type 4s courageously give up their defensive stance of proactively rejecting themselves in order to protect themselves from abandonment, they begin to integrate their "positive Shadow." They own their true goodness and accept themselves as they are. This leads them from a flawed sense of self to a realization that their inadequacy is an illusion—a strangely safe illusion, but a fantasy based on the fear of being hurt again. As they progress on their path, they come to embrace their own essential wholeness—and they become uniquely gifted in supporting others on that same journey from envy to equanimity.

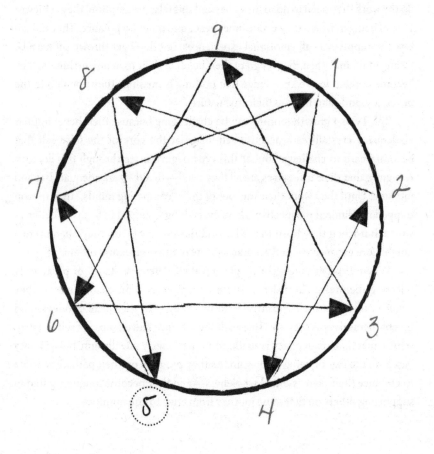

Type 5

The Path from Avarice to Nonattachment

A person is a person through other persons; you can't be a human in isolation; you are human only in relationships.

DESMOND TUTU

O nce upon a time, there was a person named Five. Five came into this world with a mission to connect deeply with everyone and everything. But at the same time, just because of the kind of person she was, she had a tendency to detach herself from others and her own heart.

When she was young, Five tried to create true heartfelt connections with people. However, those people had a tendency to invade her space when she felt like being alone. And then they weren't around when she really wanted them to be. Both intrusion and unavailability were a cause of constant concern for Five, which made it hard for her to know what to do to relate well to others, especially when she felt intruded upon or neglected. She secretly felt inadequate and different from others. Trying to find ways to connect with them just frustrated her. Again and again, people either left her when she felt she needed them or they didn't allow her to be alone enough. As time went on, Five finally gave up and disconnected more and more from others and from her feelings.

Five found she felt calm and comfortable when she spent time by herself. And this feeling grew stronger as time went by. Eventually, Five lost her ability to connect with people when she wanted to. And because of all the time she spent alone, she forgot how to let them know when she wanted to get closer to them or when she missed them. To avoid the frustration she had felt before, she decided to wait for others to notice when she felt alone—which, unfortunately, almost never happened. As she grew older, without really realizing it, Five forgot about her fundamental need for connection. She got used to being alone. She liked the comfort and safety of being by herself. It was so much easier than being with people.

Five liked learning, because it made her feel smart (and more adequate), and it was something she could do on her own. She was happy with her identity as a self-sufficient, self-contained person who knew a lot about a lot of things. She took secret pleasure in knowing things and even started feeling a little more confident because of how much she knew. She still dodged people who tried to connect with her, however, and she still wanted to avoid the pain of feeling invaded when she wanted to be alone—or of being left alone when she wanted to be with someone. She didn't want to lose the sense of safety she got from being able to live in her mind, and she didn't want to risk sharing more of herself. She also didn't want to share her books or any of her other treasured possessions.

As an adult, Five's dedication to gathering knowledge, together with her natural mental sharpness, helped her achieve a comfortable position in an area of specialization that allowed her to feel autonomous and self-sufficient. As a self-employed professional, she managed to avoid the spotlight. Each day, after doing whatever she needed to do, she dedicated time to what she loved most—learning more, hidden away in her private space.

Then one day, Five noticed that everything she did was predictable. She didn't have much energy; she didn't feel alive. She usually felt tired, especially when she was around people. She felt exhausted when others asked things of her or wanted to tell her about their feelings. After some anxious reflection, Five fell asleep. And as she slept, she dreamed. In her dream, she felt alone in a way that disturbed her. She had no motivation to study or learn. She mysteriously, almost against her will, felt an extreme amount of love for the people around her. She didn't want to be alone anymore. She wanted to be close to these people. Five felt as if her world had turned upside down, and she didn't know what to do. Then she woke up.

Five couldn't decide whether her dream had been a good experience or a nightmare. She spent some time thinking about this, but then forgot about it and went back to doing the same things she did every day—by herself.

Five had become a zombie—a private, self-contained, quiet zombie, but a zombie just the same.

The Type 5 Checklist

If most or all of the following personality traits apply to you, you may be a Type 5:

☑ You focus much of your attention on learning new things as an end in itself, not as a means to achieve something else.

☑ You consistently worry about maintaining your private space and time, and you avoid demands being made on you by the outside world.

☑ You detach to observe things and people from a distance to understand what's going on.

☑ You habitually consume more information or knowledge than the average person.

☑ You have a difficult time connecting with or staying connected to your own emotions and to other people.

☑ It's important to you that things be logical and that they make sense.

☑ You actively seek to have control over your time. You are sensitive to having to participate in interactions that last longer than the amount of time you want to give them.

☑ You believe you will be depleted if people keep asking you for things or sharing their feelings with you.

☑ You specialize in specializing. You like being an expert and going deep into areas of specific interest.

If, after using this checklist, you find that you are a Type 5 personality, your growth journey will follow three steps.

First, you will embark on a quest to know yourself by learning to identify the ways in which you disconnect from people and emotions to preserve your own space and energy.

Then you must face your Shadow to become more aware of behaviors that stem from the fact that your own knowledge and your own company don't really fulfill your emotional needs. You start to grow beyond your self-limiting personality habits by recognizing how this pattern creates a deep feeling of lack in your heart.

Finally, you can move toward the high side of your type by learning not to hoard knowledge and avoid people out of a fear of depletion. As you become more conscious of the ways you keep yourself shut off from what you need the most, you come to trust that connecting with others will be effortless once you connect more deeply with your own heart.

. . . .

"Here is my secret: I don't mind what happens."
—Jiddu Krishnamurti

. . . .

EMBARKING ON THE QUEST

The first stage of the path to awakening for this type involves consciously creating more space to become aware of their own thought patterns and noticing how they detach from their emotions. By actively observing how they deny attention and love to others when they don't feel they receive enough care and love themselves, they start to acknowledge the vicious cycle they create—a cycle that doesn't serve them.

Type 5s begin to grow beyond their self-limiting perspective when they start to develop the capacity to recognize how much attention they give to an intellectual approach to life and how little they attend to their hearts and bodies. And they must learn to see the problems their mental approach to life creates for them without judging themselves. By becoming conscious of all the ways they try to be self-sufficient and how this may arise out of a fear of being ignored, they take the first step on their path.

Key Type 5 Patterns

If you identify as a Type 5, you can launch your journey of awakening by focusing on and making more conscious these five habitual patterns.

Over-Thinking

While it is true that thought and analysis help you figure things out and gain a sense of control, it will be important for you to understand that this does not support your inner growth. The body is more than "a support for the head," and your heart is the very best compass you can have to show you what to do and how to prioritize. When you over-value reasoning, analysis, and observation, you may acquire knowledge; but you don't necessarily gain wisdom, which comes only from experience.

Fear of Connection Leading to Loneliness

You clearly don't like people to invade your space or take control of your time. Your concern about preventing this dictates many of your choices and actions. You have probably developed a capacity to feel well (or even very well) with yourself when alone. However, you most likely have a big unconscious wish to be able to connect with people more deeply. Explore how these conflicting wishes— always wanting more time alone and secretly wanting to feel more connected to people—operate in you and how they make it hard for others to relate to your "mixed messages" about how close you want them to be.

Isolating Yourself

Chances are that you see your tendency to isolate yourself physically or emotionally as a benign habit or a personal style. But this frequent movement away from others may derive from being hurt by them or fearing you will be hurt by them. Tune in to yourself at a deeper level and notice how often this fear of being hurt arises. Try to notice if you are actually much more sensitive than you may have assumed, and consider that this hypersensitivity may explain why you disconnect so much from your heart.

Fearing Abundance

You may notice that you automatically react against things when they become "too much"—when they feel too overwhelming. You may tend to withdraw when people talk too much, or when they make too many requests too often, or when they want to be too close for too long. You may be put off when there is too much of a good thing and react negatively when there is too much fun, too much enjoyment, or "too much love." Observe yourself to see if this comes from a fear of abundance and leads you to hide from potentially fulfilling experiences by taking refuge in a life script that makes you believe you don't need very much, or that it's better to live a simple, minimalistic existence.

Being Excessively Controlling and Self-Controlling

You likely take pride in being sensible and self-contained. Look to see if you have an excessive tendency to exert control over yourself in a way that removes the possibility of fun and spontaneity. While you may not typically like to control others, you may tend to be very controlling in specific ways when others are close to you. This tendency comes from a need to proactively prevent people from invading your space, occupying your time, consuming your precious energy, or messing up your plans. This habit may make your life more comfortable and predictable, but not intense or joyful. You may be pushing away the people you love without fully realizing it. You may be relying unconsciously on living a safe life that transpires mostly in your head. But by staying in your comfort zone, you are missing opportunities to experience more of the richness and depth of life that are available to you.

· ·

"Solitude matters, and for some people,
it is the air they breathe." —Susan Cain

· ·

The Type 5 Passion

Avarice is the passion that drives Type 5. As the core emotional motivation of this type, avarice manifests as closing the heart to giving and receiving. By becoming more aware of this passion, this type can make real progress on their growth journey.

The passion of avarice is not necessarily related to money, as it is often understood. According to the Enneagram teaching, avarice is related to the shutting down of the heart. Type 5s have difficulty showing up in life with an open heart and being in touch with all their emotions. Being open emotionally can be unknown territory for them, because they have learned to trust their intellect more than their feelings. Their hearts can shut down for different reasons—trauma, early unattended needs, disappointment in a love relationship, betrayal, unmet expectations, or even the difficulty of life in general. No matter the reason, they end up closing their hearts in a significant way, often becoming incapable of feeling their emotions at all. In fact, this type typically suffers from the fear of feeling.

Type 5s feel an urge to disconnect when hurt or ignored. This may happen on a number of levels: physical (not being around someone), emotional (closing the heart and feeling nothing), mental (not remembering that someone exists), and even instinctive (abruptly disconnecting from positive sensations). Moreover, they have a hard time connecting with or staying connected with others. They may just think of themselves as having a more introverted style than others, but their difficulty bonding actually reflects a deep fear of not receiving what they need from others. They may also fear being depleted if they share all they have with someone else. In fact, some 5s report having the sensation that they will be completely drained of all energy—and even of life itself—if they stay emotionally connected to others. They regularly fear that the individuals in their lives will make too many demands on them or have expectations of them (verbalized or not) that are too frequent or excessive. They also tend to feel deprived if someone with whom they want to connect doesn't give them as much as they feel they need.

In these ways, avarice can seem like a contraction against life itself. It leads this type to make themselves small in the face of all the abundant life force available and the infinite nature of the universe. In a sense, avarice can be seen as a disconnection from our limitless possibilities as human beings. This type adopts a belief in scarcity and settles for less in their lives. They tend to be good at getting by on fewer resources. And, since closing down to what's possible and the beauty of abundance in life is very sad, they also shut down their hearts so they don't feel the pain of closing down. To move forward on their growth journey, they have to allow themselves to feel the pain of disconnection and the sadness of a life without joy.

If you identify with this personality type, here are some typical manifestations of avarice that you must observe and make more conscious on your path to awakening:

- A communication pattern of speaking less and more quietly, and using neutral or nonemotional language.

- A preference for clear boundaries around time, space, and energy. A tendency to make a limited amount of energy available for interpersonal interactions, and to avoid surprises that may require more energy.

- An interest in knowledge as a way to disconnect from people and emotions.

- The tendency to miss others, but not feel the need to talk to them.

- A reluctance to speak about your own feelings or disclose personal information. Difficulty crying or connecting with emotion in the presence of others.

- A tendency to get lost in thoughts, while disconnecting from emotions or people.

- An urgent need to be alone or have private space; feeling a need to hide.

- Difficulty responding in the moment, and a tendency to delay experiencing the feelings you have when with people until later, when you are alone; a tendency to hoard your responses inside yourself.

- Detachment and a tendency to be analytical and observe what's happening from a distance while remaining contained and calm.

"To attain knowledge, add things every day. To attain wisdom, remove things every day." —Lao Tse

Using Type 5 Wings as Growth Stretches

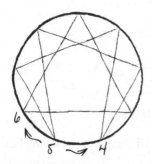

The two personality types adjacent to Type 5 on the Enneagram circle are Types 4 and 6. By expanding their emotional capacity using positive Type 4 traits, and then becoming more conscious of their fears by integrating Type 6 insights, 5s can begin to expand beyond their intellectual style and broaden their usual perspective.

- First, embody Type 4 traits by paying closer attention to your emotional states. Allow them to exist and just be. When you feel emotions, you don't need to understand them; just feel them. Allow yourself to become more spontaneous and generously self-disclosing. Add a touch of creativity to your life by initiating a project or hobby that allows you to express yourself to others, bringing what's inside you out into the world. Increase the intensity of your experience by talking at length with someone you trust about something you feel strongly about.

- Then integrate Type 6 traits by amping up your conscious connection to your fear and becoming less calm, even if you become more anxious in general. Being calm is actually a sign of avarice. It signals that your heart is shut down to experience, not necessarily that you are "at peace" in a good way. Make more space inside to feel fear or anxiety, knowing that this is part of the wisdom of the human alert system registering in your body. Access your fears (instead of coldness) to motivate your actions. Sharpen your focus on problems so you can handle them more proactively. Share your ideas and concerns before being sure about them, even to the point of bothering people by talking about what could go wrong. This may be hard, but it's potentially beneficial for people who usually detach from others and their own deeper experience of life.

> "To contemplate is to look at shadows."
> —Victor Hugo

FACING THE SHADOW

The second part of the Type 5 growth journey is all about understanding how living life from an intellectual perspective prevents a fuller engagement with important parts of the self. This type integrates shadow elements by acknowledging and owning their emotions and their capacities for connection and receiving more abundance from life. This helps them learn that their belief in scarcity holds them back from living a much fuller and more satisfying life.

At this point on their journey, Type 5s realize that their focus on being rational, logical, and sensible (which they thought was a good thing) can be a bad thing. Their lack of self-awareness allows them to become disengaged and uninterested, even while they consciously think that they have their heads in the right place. By using information and knowledge to fill in gaps in their emotional experience, they can unintentionally bypass an important stage of growth, as well as an opportunity to become more fully human. By losing touch with their emotions, they become cold and insensitive—both with themselves and with others. This part of the Type 5 path can be painful and uncomfortable because they need to become aware of and start to work against the ways they have cut themselves off from a deeper experience of life through adhering to survival strategies that have kept them safe.

Meeting the Type 5 Shadow

If you identify as a Type 5, here are some actions you can take to recognize, become more aware of, and start working against the key unconscious patterns, blind spots, and pain points of the type:

- Identify and voice your emotions in a nonrational way, making sure that you really feel your emotions and don't just think about them.

- Open up more with people. Allow them to come close to you when they want to, not just when you want them to.

- Let go of your need to control your schedule. Allow others to make more decisions about how you spend your time and be more flexible with your agenda.

- Invite people into your personal space, both into your home and into your life in general.

- Share your feelings more often, even if others are not sharing theirs.

- Break out of your self-sufficiency mode. Ask for help. Draw on other people's opinions.

- When you get tired, don't give in to your (false) belief in scarcity when it comes to how much energy you think you have. Increase the intensity you bring to whatever you do. Recognize that your energy is limited only because you think it is.

- Share your opinions about something before you think you know it all.

- Do things before planning them out completely. Allow for some improvisation and spontaneity.

. . . .

"There are many ways of going forward, but only one way of standing still." —Franklin D. Roosevelt

. . . .

The Type 5 Blind Spots

Many Type 5s may not want to examine their blind spots because they think they already know a lot about themselves. They tend to be insecure beneath the surface, and their survival strategies help them avoid feelings. As a defense against being more open to their feelings, they may operate on the assumption that they are intellectually superior to others, or they may convey this impression. They resist experiencing things by focusing inward or observing from a safe distance. By feeling most comfortable when they are alone, and playing it safe by spending so much time in their comfort zone, they block their growth by not seeing what lies beneath their desire for privacy. In zombie mode, 5s will do everything they can to avoid facing the discomfort of opening themselves up to engaging more deeply with themselves and with life.

But here's the good news. If you identify with Type 5 and are willing to look at your blind spots and feel any pain that arises, you will eventually experience a deep and wonderful sense of connection to everything, including yourself. If you can endure some discomfort as you practice staying truly present to other people—and to feelings and sensations—you will learn to enjoy more connection with others. And you may feel relief at not wanting to withdraw from others all the time.

Here are some of the central Type 5 blind spots you must make more conscious to move forward on your journey.

Intellectualizing as a Defense Mechanism

Do you try to understand and explain everything logically as a way to manage things without experiencing them directly? Do you sometimes make simple things more complicated and practical things more abstract and less manageable? Here are some things you can do to integrate this blind spot:

- Several times a day, repeat this phrase: "Emotions and sensations are to be lived, not understood."

- With a psychotherapist or close friend you trust, talk about all the ways you have felt inadequate or weird throughout your life.

- Notice what blocks you from an ongoing experience of joy.

- Consider what will happen if you allow yourself to smile and laugh more, and think and intellectualize less.

- Ask yourself what is so bad about just letting yourself experience life in its most simple yet profound moments. How do you really feel about the possibility of having more fun and lightness in your life?

- Get in touch with your avarice as it relates to knowledge. Move toward nonattachment by admitting that you don't know that much and put your knowledge into practice by applying it in your lived experience.

- Become more aware of how the fear of feeling drives your tendency to intellectualize.

- Get others to ask you to do something silly with them when you think you are getting too serious or analytical.

Learning as a Central Objective

Does learning motivate you more than anything else? Do you manage projects and relationships badly when you make learning something new your top (or only) priority? Do you get so focused on taking in more information that you fail to take action? Here are some things you can do to integrate this blind spot:

- Recognize your underlying motives whenever you take more time doing something so that you can learn more. What are you really looking for? What are the costs of this?

- Become aware of the resentment you feel when you are forced to do something you already know how to do.

- Be aware of any desire to change what you do when you don't feel intellectually challenged. Why do you always need to be so mentally active? What are the negative consequences of this?

- Admit that you may be more interested in people's ideas and information than in the people themselves. Notice how this focus keeps you from engaging with others in more meaningful ways.

- Become aware of your fear that you may have to spend your time just relating to others without learning anything. What feelings are you avoiding by focusing so much on expanding your knowledge base?

- Notice that your habits of observing, analyzing, planning, and studying all exist as methods for fulfilling your insatiable desire to learn more. Make your avarice for knowledge more conscious. Notice how it operates to keep you in your comfort zone—your head.

Failure to Communicate Clearly

Do you often receive feedback that people don't know what you are thinking or haven't heard from you? Do people sometimes tell you they don't feel you are present? Do you have difficulty sharing with others? Here are some things you can do to integrate this blind spot:

- Recognize how difficult it is for you to communicate with others in a more personal way. If you think you do this well, consider what people tell you. Admit that you don't do this as much as you could.

- Notice whether or not you are communicating effectively. Although your thoughts seem vivid to you and you may assume that you are conveying them, you may be forgetting to reach out to let others know what you are thinking—or that you thought of them.

- Observe your tendency to avoid communicating if you feel upset with someone and admit that this is not the most mature thing to do.

- Explore your tendency to focus on using the exact right words, rather than being more expressive in your facial expressions and body language. Since 80 percent of communication is nonverbal, consider how you can improve in this area.

- Notice how you communicate using either very few words or too many words. Become more aware of how you talk with people in formal, academic ways that may not be fully understood by more emotional or instinctual people.

- Get in touch with your fear of sharing more of yourself. Notice if you regularly feel scared of becoming emotionally intense or saying something silly or revealing more than you want to. Be aware of what you fear and how these fears hold you back.

- Start communicating more deeply and thoroughly with a few people you trust. Gradually do the same with more people.

. . . .

"Consider the trees which allow the birds to perch and fly
away without either inviting them to stay or desiring
they never depart. If your heart can be like this,
you will be near to the way." —Zen saying

. . . .

Type 5 Pain

This type tends to be knowledgeable and intellectually resourceful, and they create an ego identity based on these traits. Part of their survival strategy is to bypass emotions and sensations, because they subconsciously worry that they are somehow different from other people, and they tend to be fearful of being overwhelmed or depleted by emotions. While they are sometimes perceived as arrogant, they actually hide an inferiority complex behind a superiority complex. They adopt the persona of the "intellectual" or the "one who knows more" to avoid being seen as shy or unskilled at relating to others.

In order to awaken, 5s must become more aware of their tendency to hide behind their intellect as a defense—and the emotions underlying this tendency. They are naturally funny and interesting people when they decide to relax and stop worrying about being seen as awkward or strange. But they push away spontaneity out of an unconscious fear of being seen as socially or emotionally incompetent.

If you identify with this type, in order to grow beyond zombie mode you must learn to welcome any impulses you may have to do or say things before analyzing whether they are appropriate—even if this makes you feel insecure. To really liberate yourself from the habits that keep you from connecting more deeply with others, you must get more in touch with the insecurity and emotional pain behind your fears and defenses—particularly your fear that people won't stay available to you and accept your emotional needs if you open up your heart.

Here are some steps you can take to help you experience your emotions (and your pain) more deeply and more often:

- Do body work before doing emotional work. This will help you achieve a more profound and sustainable experience of opening your heart later on.

- Be aware of the void in your heart when you try to feel emotions. Pay attention to this and allow yourself to suffer when you are conscious of this void. Stay in touch with this pain so you can learn to stay in touch with your emotions. It is the gateway to owning your emotional experience.

- Notice whether you detach from people and emotions as a way to avoid your fear of feeling. This type is really good at avoiding situations in which fear may arise.

- Identify situations in your childhood that made you feel alone because no one was available to connect with you. You may have closed your heart because there was nobody there to give you what you needed to feel safe when experiencing your emotions.

- Get more in touch with the emotions from which you habitually detach, and allow yourself to feel sad about all the time you wasted being isolated and unable to connect with others. Reject the possibility of living the rest of your life with a closed heart, without being able to access your emotions and connect with others on an emotional level.

- Observe what happens when you open up more to others and become more supported by nourishing relationships. Acknowledge the happiness you feel when you allow for more abundance and love in your life. Feel the emotions that arise when people around you don't run away and you can actually connect with them and feel seen and met.

- Open your heart and make the connection that is more important and nurturing than any other—the one with yourself. Self-love is waiting for you, and it is wonderful and important.

> "I know that I know nothing."
> —Socrates

The Type 5 Subtypes

Identifying your Type 5 subtype can help you target your efforts to confront your blind spots, unconscious tendencies, and hidden pain. The specific patterns and tendencies of the subtypes vary depending on which of the three survival instincts dominates your experience.

Self-Preservation 5 Subtype

This subtype hides away from other people and builds physical boundaries, retreating into their own houses or (usually small) personal spaces. They minimize their needs to cope with the fact that living in an enclosure is not easily compatible with human relationships and that having to spend too much time in the outside world can feel dangerous. They have a need to be able to withdraw to a place of refuge when they choose to. They tend toward minimalism and find it hard to share facts about themselves and their emotions, both good and bad.

Social 5 Subtype

This subtype works to know all there is to know about a particular subject and wants to be included in the (usually small) list of experts on that topic. They may relate more to others who share their values and intellectual interests than to the people in their everyday life. They fear "not knowing" more than they fear intrusion into their private space. They appear communicative and sociable, and enjoy intellectual discussions and sharing knowledge with people, but they rely on information and knowledge to push more heart-based connections away.

Sexual (One-to-One) 5 Subtype

This subtype searches for the ideal or ultimate relationship. But they can become too picky about the people to whom they want to be close, sometimes requiring the "right person" to pass a lot of tests. They have a romantic, artistic, or imaginative streak, and a strong connection to their emotions, but they usually communicate them only indirectly through some medium of self-expression. Unlike the other Type 5 subtypes, they have a greater need for intimacy under the right circumstances—usually when they find someone they trust who will appreciate them despite their flaws.

The Type 5 Subtype Shadows

You can more effectively confront your own Shadow if you know the specific shadow characteristics of your Type 5 subtype. Below are some of the shadow aspects of each subtype. As subtype behavior can be highly automatic, these traits can be the hardest to see and own.

Self-Preservation 5 Shadow

If this is your subtype, you likely live a secretive and secluded life, but that doesn't do you as much good as you may think. You may become intolerant when your space is "invaded" by other people and keep all your personal information to yourself, but that doesn't help you develop beyond your ego limitations. By keeping yourself physically away from others, you become even more aloof and you avoid addressing your fears. Notice if you hold yourself back by minimizing what you communicate with others—and especially if you don't allow yourself to express anger and engage in conflict.

Social 5 Shadow

If this is your subtype, you always try to be and look smart and knowledgeable, but that doesn't bring you true wisdom or joy. Nor is it a humble way of life. You may treat some people differently from others, according to whether or not you view them as members of your "special group." Notice if you tend to be warmer and more available to people who have the same level of interest and expertise in your preferred subject or cause—and colder and less attentive to people who don't. You may prioritize causes and the search for knowledge and meaning above individuals out of an unconscious fear of meaninglessness, but this keeps you disconnected from people and unable to truly care about them. Your tendency to bypass emotional development in favor of purely intellectual engagement may mean you think you are more conscious than you actually are.

Sexual (One-to-One) 5 Shadow

If this is your subtype, you limit the people with whom you can connect deeply by being very selective and demanding a high level of trust in your personal relationships. While you want a high degree of intimacy with a partner, you may limit your availability for true intimacy by needing to control the relationship and exaggerating the amount of trust you require to open up. By searching for the ultimate in relationship, you may resist opportunities that life brings to connect with a wider range of regular people.

> "Never forget to smile: a day without smiling is a day lost."
> —Charles Chaplin

The Type 5 Paradox

The Type 5 paradox is experienced through the polarity between the passion of avarice and the virtue of nonattachment. Nonattachment is a state of being totally open to the natural flow of life force, receiving all of it, not hoarding it inside, and giving it back to the world by opening up more to the people around you. For this type, recognizing how they disconnect from people, emotions, and life itself allows them to acknowledge a central aspect of their passion. They grow when they see the disparity between their bright, sophisticated minds and their childish, undeveloped hearts. When they can observe themselves hurting others by being cold and detached from their emotions, they learn to recognize their avarice.

If you identify as a Type 5, you can make progress on the path toward nonattachment by becoming more aware of how avarice operates. In a state of nonattachment, you reconnect with all there is to experience in life from an open heart and learn to allow everything to arise naturally without disconnecting or shutting down. You come to experience the mysteries and joys of life without having to hide or control what's happening. You learn to let go instead of withholding your energy or hoarding your past experiences in your heart.

Here are some first steps you can take toward becoming more conscious of your avarice and accessing the higher-level emotion of nonattachment:

- Recognize when you feel a need to shut down your heart. Take the risk of being a little bit more open.

- Notice when you act from avarice, but don't judge yourself. Ask yourself what keeps you from staying connected in the present moment.

- Have compassion for the part of you that needs to protect your heart from hurt and lack of attention from others. Allow yourself to stay in touch with whatever feelings arise, as opposed to ignoring them or only thinking about your feelings instead of really feeling them.

- Recognize when you lower your energy level and end up feeling less in touch with your capacity for intensity. Catch yourself in the act of giving up on the possibility of experiencing a zest for life.

- Become aware of your disconnection from your body and the way you tend to experience life automatically through purely mental experiences ungrounded in your emotions or your body.

- Get in touch with the radical separation you impose between people, groups, and situations. Notice how you compartmentalize, thereby restricting your experience of all there is around you from a state of presence.

. . . .

"Life force energy is miraculously ever so abundant,
so dig in." —Shumlosh

. . . .

Using Type 5 Arrow Lines for Growth

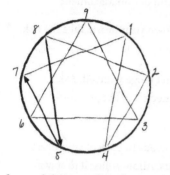

The two types connected to Type 5 by the arrow lines within the Enneagram diagram are Types 7 and 8. By integrating Type 8's capacity for action, this type can develop their energy and intensity; by applying Type 7's insights, they can increase their ability to be spontaneous, flexible, and open-minded. This helps them create a radical growth shift by moving them beyond their usual tendency to concentrate more on reason than experience.

- First, draw on Type 8's strength to ground yourself strongly in your whole body and not just your head. Breathe into your belly and focus your attention on your physical presence. Quiet your mind and get more in touch with bodily sensations. Allow yourself to feel anger and use that anger as energy, power, and drive. Let it fuel a feeling of self-confidence to become more practical and effective. Embody your power and authority by asserting yourself more forcefully and taking action more quickly and more often to balance your cerebral style. When you feel strongly about something, let people know.

- Then integrate Type 7's tendency to be more adventurous, quick-witted, fun, happy, spontaneous, flexible, and creative. Learn to experiment more with ideas and to take action or speak out before you finish gathering information. Expand more outside yourself by sharing activities that excite you with others. Create more balance between the "inside" and "outside" by socializing more. Allow yourself to be motivated by a desire for pleasure, rather than a hunger for knowledge.

"Wealth is the ability to fully experience life."
—Henry David Thoreau

Embracing the High Side

On the third part of their journey, this type begins to see more clearly who they are *not*. They separate more from their false selves and start to embody their true selves. By opening up their hearts for giving and receiving more freely without controlling the flow of energy, they can access more vitality in a way that allows them to be much more intense. When they are more energized, they can connect more deeply to others, to themselves, and to life.

If you are a Type 5, this awakening involves learning to be more practical, simple, direct, and decisive. You see the people around you more clearly as who they are; you empathize with others more; you consider their needs more. When you become conscious of your avarice and stop trying to over-think things, life gets better. You stop feeling the need to protect your space, your time, and your energy. Best of all, you feel joyfully alive and understand that your energy will not be depleted if you share yourself and your resources with others. You finally recognize the falsity of your belief in scarcity.

Here are some things you can do on this part of your journey that you couldn't have done before—and what you can continue to work on:

- Feel invigorated and unconcerned about hoarding time, energy, and other resources.

- Stop avoiding situations in which other people may make demands on you—which could include just wanting to know more about you.

- Feel more joyful in general.

- Stop detaching from emotions and other people. Stop withdrawing from others or feeling the need to hide.

- Allow yourself to experience a feeling of strength and presence in your body and in your heart.

- Be more regularly present and connected to people and to the flow of life.

- Experience great improvement in the quality of all your relationships.

- Understand things, not only through your intellect, but also from an embodied sense of being. Access other forms of knowledge, including emotion and intuition.

- See the abundant love, support, and nourishment available to you, and be able to welcome and enjoy more and deeper contact with the people around you who care about you.

> "It is only by experience that we find out how hard it is to attain the state of nonattachment." —Mahatma Gandhi

The Type 5 Virtue

Nonattachment is the virtue that provides an antidote to the Type 5 passion of avarice. In nonattachment, this type gladly opens up to feeling their emotions when others come close to them to give them attention and love. They move closer to others more easily. They learn to act from their hearts and to live in a more embodied way. They feel connected to everything and everyone, and are not afraid to occupy their bodies and own their feelings. They feel energized by more ongoing contact with their own life force and live more fully with joy and less planning. They break away from the belief that their own energy is limited so they can give more to others without hoarding.

When 5s achieve a state of nonattachment—not only to space, time, and energy, but also to knowledge—they live from a remembrance of their real selves and realize that they don't need to know everything. They recognize that storing knowledge inside themselves is pointless. They come to know that they can access all the information and wisdom they need by connecting to a universal database of intuitive knowing that is available to all of us when we are in touch with our higher selves.

The state of nonattachment is characterized by an experience of love, unity, and connection with other people and with the universe. We experience this state, not in our heads, but in our hearts. It's a state of connectedness with all of reality in which we realize we are all interconnected, interdependent, and intrinsically inseparable. This means that we can stop seeking privacy and isolation, and stop disconnecting from our hearts, from people, or from the immense flow of life all around us. We can give more of ourselves to others more generously.

It is important here to clearly differentiate the state of "nonattachment" from the state of "detachment." Nonattachment is a state in which the heart is totally open. Detachment is a part of the deadened state of the false self. The Type 5 ego drives 5s to detach and disconnect from feelings and people by shutting down the emotions and the possibility of connecting with others. But nonattachment helps them to wake up and reanimate by encouraging a more courageous openness to real feelings and connections without fear of being overwhelmed or feeling empty.

If you identify as a Type 5, here are some actions you can take to work against the tendencies fueled by avarice. By taking these steps, you can live more from a state of nonattachment:

- Overcome the fear of not receiving enough from those you expect to give you attention, care, and love.

- Resist expecting things from people and try not to disconnect from them. Stay completely open for an authentic, mutual exchange.

- Approach people on your own initiative, with a true sense of openness. Encounter others, not only from your head, but also from your heart and your gut, so you can fully participate in emotional and sensory interactions.

- Be present to whatever is happening and whoever is with you in the moment. Let yourself be loved abundantly or left alone in solitude, without closing down to experiencing life as it comes.

- Be willing and open to receive whatever life brings you, without trying to control what happens. Go with the flow of whatever occurs in your life without needing to plan ahead.

- Connect with your life force more fully and actively develop more zest for life.

- Let go of the need to demonstrate that you know everything by appreciating the humility of not knowing and valuing the experience of the simpler things in life.

- Let go of your need to hoard things and experiences. Resist your tendency to retreat. Realize that withdrawing makes you feel safe, but prevents you from feeling fulfillment.

- Bravely stay open to experiencing the natural flow of whatever is happening in life without needing to contract or withhold in the face of either lack or abundance.

. . . .
"If we fearfully cling to what we have, we will never be able to discover who we truly are." —Sri Chinmoy
. . . .

Waking Up from the Zombie State

For Type 5s, the key to embracing their true selves lies in gradually reducing their need to be in control of others' movements either toward or away from them. This may seem difficult, if not impossible, for them, because their ego tells them not to open the gates to their domain. But facing their Shadow and their pain means rising above their self-limiting definitions of the past and achieving a higher degree of self-knowledge and self-respect, as well as a wider vision of who they are.

When this type realizes that they have actually been missing deeper and freer connections for much of their life, they can focus all their intention and attention on exchanging ideas, feelings, and sensations with others. It is only through fully engaging in the experience of connection that they can develop their true selves and understand the mysteries of being human, living life, and being part of the universe. When they take in this truth, they blossom and make themselves available to others with a profound spirit of generosity. And this brings them closer to their true selves.

The Type 5 journey can be challenging, because many cultures value the intellect and promote ideals of individuality, self-sufficiency, and privacy. And when this type feels "in control" of their space and their agenda, they may not feel the need for the change that comes through growth. But the truth is that avarice—the impulse to contract against life out of a sense of scarce inner resources—shrinks the heart and makes life less interesting. Knowledge doesn't make up for the lost experience of living more fully. And moving through the world as a Type 5 zombie means living only half of a life—if even this much. When 5s courageously examine themselves, face their shadows, and open up to the unknown, they wake up out of their unconscious ego-driven zombie state and gain true wisdom.

This type has a deep craving for wisdom. This makes sense, given that their main survival strategy relies on knowing all there is to know. But this desire compels them to observe life from a distance and trade felt experience for a cognitive understanding of life. As they advance on their path, however, they discover what it means to develop real wisdom. When this happens, they open up to a more satisfying experience of knowing that comes through a deep engagement of the body, mind, heart, and spirit. When they allow for the lived experiences that make them truly wise and not just smart, they come to a realization of true humility. From this lived humility, they unveil more knowledge, but also know they know nothing. And this paves the way for them to align with the higher self that has been waiting for them all along.

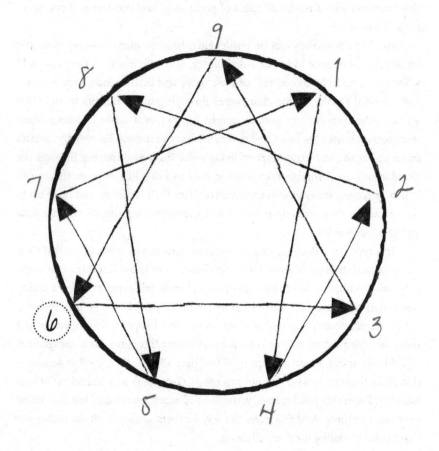

Type 6

The Path from Fear to Courage

Don't be afraid of your fears. They're not there to scare you.
They're there to let you know that something is worth it.

C. JoyBell C.

O nce upon a time, there was a person named Six. She came into this life with a singular capacity to be courageous, but also with a tendency to experience herself as smaller and more fearful than she actually was. When she was a very young child, Six was happy and free. She did what she wanted without thinking about it too much. She didn't plan ahead and she didn't allow any fear of the dangers of the world to distract her from enjoying life and having fun. She had many friends and enjoyed learning and exploring. She even took tests calmly and with confidence.

As Six grew up, however, she had a few experiences that made her feel afraid. Her mother once forgot to pick her up at school. She was frightened by a movie that showed people being killed. She started noticing all the things that could go wrong and learned that sometimes bad things happened. The world started seeming more dangerous and more threatening to her.

One day, Six got very anxious about her performance on a test. She got so worried that she imagined she was getting every answer wrong. Because this picture of certain failure was so vivid in her head, she froze. And indeed, she did very badly on the test. Around the same time, she started being suspicious of people and wondering if they could be trusted. Then she had a few more bad experiences that made her feel very angry, but also very scared.

As Six grew older, she started doubting the intentions of some of her old friends. Did they really like her? Then she began to have paranoid thoughts about some of her new friends. Were they out to get her? Were they just waiting for her to trust them so they could do something bad to her? As her fears and doubts grew, she imagined all the bad things that could possibly happen to her. What if someone stole her money? What if her parents died in a car accident and she was left all alone? What if her cat got lost or her dog got hurt? What if she caught a strange disease? Six became paralyzed with fear and doubt. She wanted to feel safe and carefree as she had before, but that didn't seem possible. The world seemed like a fundamentally dangerous place. The only thing that seemed to help was to imagine all the bad things that *could* happen, so that she could make sure they didn't. But any feeling of safety that brought her was only temporary.

Six tried to address the threats she perceived by preparing for the worst, and this became a big part of her survival strategy. But even though she was very inventive and resourceful when imagining all the things that could go wrong and what she would do if they did, she was still consumed by her fearful thoughts. Soon, she was nearly always preoccupied with planning what she would do if her fears came true. And this only made things worse.

The need to feel safe in what seemed to her like an obviously dangerous world drove Six to try to manage all the many threats in her environment. It was exhausting, but she couldn't stop going around in circles in her head. She had to be on top of security. Safety first! And always. She got a first aid kit. She studied harder so she would never do badly on a test again. Her survival strategy was out of control. She could imagine fearful things that were about to happen everywhere. And she couldn't stop imagining different kinds of threats or suspecting the shifty-looking people all around her. She watched them to find clues about their ulterior motives, their hidden agendas, and their bad intentions. She knew they were up to something.

Six had become a zombie—an intensely cautious, hardworking, and security-minded zombie, but a zombie just the same.

The Type 6 Checklist

If most or all of the following personality traits apply to you, you may be a Type 6:

- ☑ You focus much of your attention on risks, dangers, or threats. You allow about 20 percent of actual risks to occupy 80 percent of your thoughts.

- ☑ You worry about not anticipating potential hazards. You try to forecast all potential problems so you can either prevent them or be prepared to manage them.

- ☑ You automatically question what is said and say the opposite. (Was your first reaction when you read this to argue against it?)

- ☑ You habitually stay vigilant so you can scan for potential problems. This makes you feel more tense and anxious than most people.

- ☑ You have a difficult time trusting others—and sometimes even trusting yourself.

- ☑ You try to increase your sense of certainty by questioning what's happening.

- ☑ You try to control what actually does happen by imagining what might happen before you take action.

- ☑ You believe that, unless you mentally elaborate worst-case scenarios, you won't feel adequately prepared for them.

- ☑ When something bad actually does happen, you tend to feel calm and competent, or suddenly courageous.

If, after using this checklist, you find that you are likely a Type 6 personality, your growth journey will follow three steps.

First, you will embark on the quest to know yourself by becoming aware that you often see hidden risks that others don't and raise concerns about them.

Then you must face your Shadow by becoming more aware of the unconscious behaviors that stem from your need for security. This helps you recognize how you tend to become overwhelmed by taking responsibility and addressing problems—and how anxious you become when you imagine (or fear) the worst.

The final stage of your journey involves learning to relax, to trust life, and to move forward more confidently, even when experiencing fear or facing actual risks and threats.

. . . .
"The brave man is not he who does not feel afraid, but he who conquers that fear." —Nelson Mandela
. . . .

EMBARKING ON THE QUEST

The first stage of awakening for this type involves intentionally noticing how much they are driven by fear-based fantasies. This helps them to increase their capacity to study their own fear-fueled thinking patterns and recognize—without judging—how much attention they place on maintaining a sense of security or certainty in a world they view as dangerous. They begin to notice all the ways they over-think potential problems and how they get caught in analysis paralysis.

This type works to stay alert to the dangers of the world. But the truth is, if you identify as a 6, your constant need to stay vigilant keeps you stuck in patterns dictated by fear in a way you may not see as coming from fear. You may just think you are really good at being prepared or that you have a strong sense of responsibility. Ironically, you may have become trapped in your own survival strategy in a way that perpetuates your sense of anxiety and insecurity out of a need to stay safe and feel secure. But if you want to make progress on your growth path, you must observe the way this happens, face your fears as fears, and learn new ways to overcome them.

Key Type 6 Patterns

If you identify as a Type 6, you can launch your journey of awakening by focusing on, observing, and making more conscious these five habitual patterns.

Needing Security

Notice if you have a constant need to feel safe and believe that something really bad will happen if you don't stay vigilant. Observe yourself to see if prioritize security and safety. Learn to recognize how you think and feel, and what you do when you don't feel secure. When you feel unsafe, you may tend to feel a sense of internal tension. This tension may remain unconscious, but you must work to make it more conscious. When you do manage to feel safe, try to relax and project a sense of calm, then notice if this feeling is temporary, especially if you quickly focus on the next problem to be solved.

Needing to Manage Risks

You probably excel at risk management and map out threats all the time. It will be important for you to see how you use your imagination and intellect to think about all the possible dangers that exist in a given situation, then gather data, observe, analyze, study, question, and test people in an effort to develop some sense of control over the risks you detect. While managing risks may create anxiety in you, you try to find a sense of peace or security by preparing for every possible thing that could go wrong. But this may backfire and make you more anxious, as thinking about problems keeps you focused on what's problematic, which may increase your stress. Because you are a good problem-solver, you may also be a problem-seeker.

Needing to Feel Prepared

Your central concern with what could happen leads you to do your best to be prepared so you can try to manage outcomes. This makes you good at mapping out different scenarios and preparing for them so you can deal with any problems that may arise. You may assume that, the more you prepare, the more secure you will feel. But it will be important for you to observe if your need to be prepared for the worst means you never finish getting ready to meet the next problem—and may never feel completely secure.

Testing People and Circumstances

You likely seek to build relationships you can trust, but before you can actually develop trust, you may do a lot of testing to see if it's actually safe to trust. Observe yourself to see if it feels unnatural and scary for you to trust someone if you don't have enough information about them. Do you watch people closely, looking for inconsistencies? Do they do what they say they are going to do? Do their actions align with their stated values and intentions? Notice whether, when you automatically stay vigilant, people earn your trust or reveal hidden agendas. You may pride yourself on seeing through falsehoods and false personas. Your caution related to trust may mean that you try to discover bad intentions and sometimes imagine problems that don't really exist.

Having Problems with Authority

If you are a Type 6, you will tend to have more problems with authority than the average person. Notice whether you have a sensitive antenna for detecting power dynamics. If you find this is true, your issues with authority can take different shapes. You may question people in positions of authority and take a lot of time establishing trust in them. You may initially seek to trust a person in authority out of a desire to be protected by a good authority figure, but get suspicious later. You may rebel against authority and play a contrarian role. Notice if you tend to confront authorities to protect "underdogs," whether people or causes. You may sometimes fear that trusting an authority figure too much will make you unsafe. You likely avoid being in positions of authority yourself and feel uncomfortable in leadership roles.

> "You cannot swim for new horizons until you have courage to lose sight of the shore." —William Faulkner

The Type 6 Passion

Fear is the passion that drives Type 6. As the core emotional motivation of this type, fear is the "shaky" state of the heart that accompanies an intolerance of uncertainty and arises as a reaction to the possibility of bad things happening. This type is perhaps more prone to fear because they tend to focus attention on anticipating and preparing to meet any threat that may arise through their need to cope with the unknown.

Of course, we all feel fear. And we each fear specific things. But 6s experience a more generalized sense of fear, and they keep searching for the source of that fear until they find it. In fact, for them, fear precedes whatever person or situation may be responsible for it. This type actually *projects* fear onto different people and things in their environment. They feel different kinds of fear, even when these fears are not based on a specific source or cause. They even fear fear itself. They may question why they feel so much fear. They may even be afraid of not feeling fear—for instance, if they fear there may be something dangerous on the horizon that they have not yet spotted.

Type 6 fear exists as a constant emotional state of the heart, not just an emotion that leads to particular behaviors at specific moments. Most of their fear does not result from something objective—an experience of something actually happening. Much of the time, it is based on subjective perceptions of what *might* happen. Moreover, they may not recognize fear as fear. They may just think they excel at being prepared or solving problems. For all of us, the passion that drives our type tends to be mostly unconscious until we work to become aware of how it operates. So 6s may not have named what drives them as fear. As a consequence, their fear becomes even more habitual and they find it hard to relax. The challenge for them is to recognize and feel their fear fully instead of avoiding it, and then develop more confidence in their own power to master it.

Fear generates anxiety for this type, along with constant emotional and physical tension. It can also lead to a lack of self-confidence. If you identify as a Type 6, fear may impair your view of reality, make decisions difficult, and lead to procrastination. As you become more familiar with your experience of fear, however, you can also begin to cultivate the courage it takes to move forward even when you feel scared. The more aware you become of your fear and decide not to let it hold you back, the more you manifest the higher opposite experience of courage.

If you are a Type 6, here are some typical manifestations of fear that you must make conscious to move forward on your path to awakening.

- Contrarian thinking—going against what other people say or even your own thoughts.

- Using language that conveys the uncertainty and context-dependent nature of everything—"what if" and " it depends." Answering questions with other questions.

- Procrastination; continually coming up with doubts (including self-doubt) that delay your action and your success.

- Predicting bad things that might happen to give yourself a false sense of control.

- Being surprised or concerned when good things happen. Expecting bad things to happen. ("Waiting for the other shoe to drop.")

- Scanning for danger. Horizontal eye movements. A feeling of tension in your body.

- Being excessively responsible and dedicated to managing problems. Being extra loyal to people to justify seeing them as trustworthy.

- Imagining multiple scenarios in an effort to eliminate uncertainty in a world where this is impossible.

- Being a problem-solver who constantly looks for problems to solve—and always finds them.

. . . .

"Avoiding danger is no safer in the long run than outright
exposure. The fearful are caught as often as the bold."
—Helen Keller

. . . .

Using Type 6 Wings as Growth Stretches

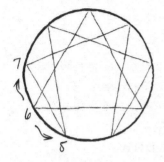

The two types adjacent to Type 6 on the Enneagram circle are Types 5 and 7. This type can ease their sense of anxiety and become more objective in the face of fear by leaning into Type 5's ability to remain calm and measured. They can then moderate their tendency to be worried and cautious by integrating Type 7's tendency to be more positive and spontaneous. This helps them move beyond their narrow focus on fears and threats and broaden their usual perspective.

- First, consciously "lean into" Type 5's ability to calm down and see things from a broader, less emotional (actively fearful) perspective. This can help you lower your anxiety level by doing a deeper investigation of the data and doing more neutral research to see what's true. Do a "reality check" on what scares you by looking more objectively at the evidence that confirms or rejects the scenarios you imagine. Stop projecting your fears onto the outside world by owning your authority to discern what's real. Enjoy taking on the role of authority (or "expert") and feel more secure by developing a greater mastery of the information connected to your intellectual interests (or what might scare you).

- Then integrate Type 7 strengths by venturing out more, exploring the world, having more fun, and being more spontaneous. Allow yourself to be more lighthearted. Relax, let go of worries or tension, and focus more on what brings you pleasure. Just move into action without feeling the need to prepare so much beforehand. Adopt a more positive attitude, and look for opportunities as much as or more than you scan for threats. Gain more flexibility and confidence by preparing less and letting yourself "wing it" more—"fake it 'til you make it"—the way Type 7s do.

"Staying vulnerable is a risk we have to take if we want to experience connection." —Brené Brown

FACING THE SHADOW

The second part of the Type 6 growth journey is all about acknowledging, accepting, and integrating the ways fear drives them and shapes the way they navigate through life. This helps them become more in touch with their strength, confidence, faith, and courage.

In this more advanced stage of their journey, this type realizes that their focus on staying safe and having a more predictable life (which they thought was a good thing) can actually be a bad thing. When they lack self-awareness, 6s can limit or sabotage themselves in ways they don't see, even while they consciously think they are just doing what's sensible and reasonable. When they ignore their blind spots and put a negative spin on everything, they may cast blame on innocent bystanders, or relentlessly accuse and doubt themselves. When they don't see and own how much fear fuels what they think and do, they can be unfair or even paranoid about other people's motives—and unaware of their own.

Meeting the Type 6 Shadow

If you identify as a Type 6, here are some actions you can take to bring to the surface, become more aware of, and start working to counteract the key unconscious patterns, blind spots, and pain points of this type:

- Identify ways your vigilance and anxiety manifest mentally, emotionally, and physically. Understand how your watchfulness works against your inner growth.

- Learn to identify and relax the tension you hold in your body that comes from fear and anxiety.

- Notice how overactive your mind is. Recognize how it looks for bad things because of its "negativity bias." Focus on seeing good things as much as you see bad things.

- Focus less on mapping out risks and worst-case scenarios, and more on identifying positive possibilities.

- Make lists of the good things that happen to you. Confront your belief that bad things always happen.

- Become aware of your tendency to create self-fulfilling prophecies— instances when you expect something bad will happen—and explore how that expectation somehow manifests itself.

- Notice how your habit of procrastination slows you down or limits you. Feel sad about the time wasted.

- Take on leadership positions without hesitating or hiding behind others. Own your power instead of projecting it onto others. Learn to be more decisive.

- Identify moments of hardship in your life when you were brave, strong, and effective. Own how strong you really were and are.

. . . .

"You don't find light by avoiding the darkness."
—S. Kelley Harrell

. . . .

The Type 6 Blind Spots

This type may not want to examine their blind spots because, while they may not "like" their anxiety, it gives them a (false) sense of security. They believe that thinking about the worst enables them to avoid it. They may feel deeply tired about having to be so watchful, but their survival strategies kick in to keep them from relaxing their vigilance. By maintaining their fearful stance all the time, however, they block their growth by not recognizing what lies beneath their constant need for protection.

But here's the good news if you identify with this type. If you can look at your blind spots and inquire into your fears—if you can acknowledge what you avoid seeing in yourself when you put all your focus on coping with danger—you will eventually experience true courage and faith. If you can face your fears and stop thinking about preparing for the worst, you will feel a lot of relief at not having to be anxious all the time.

Here are some of the specific habitual patterns that operate as blind spots that you must confront as a Type 6.

Becoming Accustomed to Stress and Fear

Do you constantly feel stressed out? Have you become used to an inner state of tension that harms you more than helps you? Does fear motivate everything you do? Here are some actions you can take to integrate this blind spot:

- Become more aware of how fear and anxiety negatively influence the ways you perceive and evaluate the situations you face in your life every day.

- Several times a day, repeat this phrase: "I can relax and still be strong and protected."

- With a psychotherapist or close friend you trust, talk about your current worries, anxieties, and fears—and your main strategies for coping with them.

- Notice what blocks you from an ongoing experience of trust in life, in others, and mainly in yourself. What do you fear will happen if you relax your vigilance? What unconscious beliefs fuel your fear and anxiety the most? Imagine how will you feel when you achieve a state of peace and calm. What do you need to do to achieve that?

- Acknowledge that, when you move toward the unknown with confidence and decisiveness, your fear disappears.

- Ask others to point out when you are projecting—imagining something scary is happening outside you when it isn't.

Not Seeing What May *Not* Go Wrong

While you are good at mapping out risks, do you also see the good things that may happen? Do you forget good things that have already happened? Here are some things you can do to integrate this blind spot:

- Recognize your underlying motives every time you think of a worst-case scenario. Mentally generate more "best-case" scenarios.

- Explore the "magical thinking" behind your belief that, if you can think of all the negative possibilities, nothing bad will happen.

- Become more conscious of your fear of expecting positive things to happen or acknowledging the positive things that do happen.

- Notice your fear of being all you can be. Consider all the ways you resist making progress and achieving success.

- Become aware of how hard it is for you to own your power and authority. How can you commit to being bolder and taking the lead in your own life?

- Recognize that, by living from fear in such a central way, you don't make room for other important human emotions, including happiness, contentment, and joy.

Failing to Own Your Own Power

Do people see you as competent and strong, but you don't really believe it? What do you think accounts for this difference in perceptions? Here are some ways you can confront this blind spot:

- Recognize that your zombie ego likes it when you stay small and don't feel ready or able. Notice how you stay comfortable by avoiding challenges or questioning yourself.

- Become aware of all the ways you project your power onto outside authorities.

- Explore why you find it hard to own your competence. Why do you fear success? Envision getting what you want and notice what feelings arise.

- Explore the reasons why you procrastinate. Do you feel more confident when you take action?

- Examine your tendency to focus on what you don't yet know. Recognize this as a delay tactic.

- Announce to close friends the date you will initiate an ambitious new plan and ask for their support.

> "The sacrifice we resist the most is the sacrifice of our own suffering." —Sufi saying

Type 6 Pain

To fully face their Shadow, Type 6s must learn to feel the pain they have avoided. The problem for this type, however, is that they don't exactly look as if they avoid pain and suffering. Others may perceive them as negative or pessimistic, but they usually describe themselves as realistic, claiming that they try to predict what will happen so they can prepare for it in advance. But their continual focus on imagining the worst means that they usually don't avoid a certain kind of discomfort.

This type's habit of dwelling in fear (or automatic reactions to fear) makes them tolerate a specific form of pain—the pain that comes from uncertainty, doubt, and insecurity in the face of danger—and not question it. Because they focus so much on fear-based coping strategies, they may not leave much space for consciously engaging and working through some of their painful emotions, like anger, insecurity, shame, or even fear itself. While they vary in how much they feel their fear—and whether or not they name what they experience as fear—they don't exactly avoid pain in the same ways that other types do.

Type 6s suffer when they don't know what will happen next. They suffer from fear of the unknown. They suffer when they envision all the threats that could materialize. They suffer when they feel a lack of protection. They suffer when they perceive others as reckless or inconsistent. They suffer when they feel the need to be on "high alert" all the time. And strangely, they suffer when good things happen, because they worry that something bad must be about to happen next. But, because they avoid or discharge their anxiety through different coping strategies, even when they consciously experience some version of fear-based suffering, they may not be aware of it in a way that allows them to move through it and release it at a deeper level. The deeper suffering they avoid—the suffering they need to invite in as part of their growth journey—could help them neutralize their low-level, ever-present anxiety. But to do this, they have to dive into the unknown, despite the fear and pain this triggers in them.

If you identify with Type 6, you must acknowledge the actual lack of protection that you experienced early in life, ideally in some sort of safe therapeutic setting. Only when you do this will you be able to see and understand how you may be reliving those earlier events over and over. You must learn to tolerate specific painful feelings to enable a fuller realization of your true self. These feelings include:

- Exhaustion from carrying the weight of being responsible for everybody and everything in life for so long.

- Regret for doubting people who actually were trustworthy. Think about times when you have misjudged people out of fear. Allow yourself to feel regret about this, but don't judge yourself.

- Shame about experiences early in life in which you were mistreated or not protected. When this happens to children, they unconsciously take on a sense of "inner badness" to protect their feelings about someone they relied on to survive, blaming themselves rather than seeing their protector as bad. Feel this consciously, but then work to let it go and own your goodness.

- Confusion from a distorted view of yourself and the world. When you feel fear, it may sometimes be hard to know what is real—whether you are intuiting real danger or making it up and projecting it onto some external person or thing. Learn when to trust yourself and when to mistrust your conclusions when you feel caught by fear or paranoid tendencies.

- Anger or aggression that comes from fear. This may be a rare occurrence or a frequent experience depending on your subtype. Become more aware of your relationship to anger and learn to channel it in healthy ways. Learn if you get angry as a response to fear or if you avoid anger altogether because of fear.

- Self-doubt rooted in a sense of responsibility, your vivid imagination, or an inability to trust in yourself and own your power. Call this self-doubt what it really is: fear of life and fear of being all you can be.

Allow yourself to explore your self-doubt fully—its sources, the ways you act it out, the ways it drives you, and its consequences. Let yourself feel it in a conscious way so that you can learn to deal with and manage it in effective, self-aware ways.

- Fear that may come from an early experience in life in which you have become stuck. Allow yourself to explore this, fully face what happened and how you felt, and then consciously draw on an experience of inner strength to move beyond it.

- Happiness, contentedness, or joy for which you don't leave much room in your life because you spend so much time focused on threats and risks.

"Being vulnerable is the only way to allow your heart to feel true pleasure." —Bob Marley

The Type 6 Subtypes

Identifying your Type 6 subtype can help you more precisely target your efforts to confront your blind spots, unconscious tendencies, and hidden pain. The specific patterns and tendencies of the subtypes vary depending on which of the three survival instincts dominates your experience.

Self-Preservation 6 Subtype

This subtype is warm and friendly. They disguise their fear by being soft and kind, and not aggressive. They feel fear as separation anxiety and try to attract strong protectors and allies to feel more protected. They are actively fearful and often "phobic," running away from danger (flight, not fight). They experience the most doubt and uncertainty, and trust others more than themselves. They are the most fearful of being angry, and they hesitate the most and ask the most questions. But they don't answer any.

Social 6 Subtype

This subtype copes with fear by finding a good authority. They think the way to be safe is to follow the rules of their chosen authority, whether a person, a system, or an ideology. They tend to be dutiful, legalistic, intellectual, responsible, and efficient, and they rely on following guidelines or reference points to feel secure. For them, uncertainty and ambiguity equal anxiety. They display a mixture of "phobic" (fearful) and "counterphobic" (confronting fear with strength) behaviors. They see the world in terms of black and white, rather than gray.

Sexual (One-to-One) 6 Subtype

This subtype is more confrontational, intense, and intimidating. They respond to fear by expressing anger. For them, the best defense is a good offense. They come across as strong and they usually don't feel or express their own fear or vulnerability. Although fear drives their behaviors, it tends to be more unconscious. They are "counterphobic" and move against perceived danger from a position of strength. At times, this gives them the appearance of rebels, risk-takers, adrenaline junkies, or troublemakers.

The Type 6 Subtype Shadows

You can more effectively confront your own Shadow if you know the specific shadow characteristics of your Type 6 subtype. Below are some of the shadow aspects of each subtype. As subtype behavior can be highly automatic, these traits can be the hardest to see and own.

Self-Preservation 6 Shadow

If this is your subtype, your way of coping with fear makes you dependent on others for protection. You keep people from attacking you by appearing nice, warm, and friendly. To feel safe, you may want to run away from situations that make you fearful. You may fear others' aggression and not feel comfortable expressing yours. You can get lost in doubt and uncertainty. While you want to feel certain, you doubt everything (even your doubt), which makes making decisions and taking action difficult. You will tend to have a hard time owning your power and authority.

Social 6 Shadow

If this is your subtype, you tend to take on a large amount of responsibility. You tend to feel duty-bound to take care of others and the collective. Loyalty to causes and authority figures may come from an egoic need to feel safe. You can become too much of a "true believer"—too devoted to authorities or ideologies. You must learn to trust your own authority, not just look outside yourself for guidelines about what to do to feel a sense of security. By focusing on systems, ideals, and rules, you may neglect your need to connect more deeply with your emotions or instincts. Go more with your heart or your gut, and not just your head.

Sexual (One-to-One) 6 Shadow

If this is your subtype, you act from fear, not courage, when you move toward risks and express strength and aggression. You intimidate others as a way of coping with fear and to ward off attacks. You need to get in touch with the fear under your strong exterior to develop real courage. You must develop more emotional strength to tolerate the experience of feeling vulnerable to become more grounded and aware. To be more conscious in your life and relationships, you need to explore your tendencies to be contrarian, controversial, thrill-seeking, and rebellious.

"What makes you vulnerable makes you beautiful."
—Brené Brown

The Type 6 Paradox

The Type 6 paradox arises from the polarity between the passion of fear and the virtue of courage. Being courageous means moving forward despite unpredictability. By becoming aware of all the ways fear operates, this type opens up to experimenting with new ways of living and develops the capacity to go into action with their hearts open—which, in turn, allows them to feel more peace and self-confidence. They stop trying to be certain about everything before doing things and feel more connected to their bodies and their hearts. They develop the ability to move out of their heads at will and feel guided by faith instead of fear.

If you identify as a Type 6, here are some steps you can take to become more conscious of your fear and access the higher-level emotion of courage:

- Recognize when you feel anxious and crave predictability. Relax and see all the good things that are happening (and that will probably continue to happen).

- Notice the pressure that arises when you get close to putting your plans into action. Notice your tendency to analyze or rehearse. Shorten your timeline and go into action despite your anxiety.

- Have compassion for the part of you that needs to feel safe. Get in touch with the emotions you experience when you feel threatened.

- Acknowledge when you act from fear, but don't judge yourself. Breathe more consciously, slowly, and calmly. Come back to the present moment instead of thinking of all the bad things that could happen.

- Become aware of the exhaustion you feel as a consequence of over-analyzing potential problems and hazards. Feel into the relief you experience when you intentionally allow yourself to relax.

- Focus more attention on your body. Engage in some form of movement or exercise to move your attention to your physical body so you feel more grounded and confident.

- Next time you feel afraid of doing something—or hesitate to go into action—feel your fear and push yourself forward. If this is challenging, ask a friend to push you. As you move forward, notice what courage feels like.

> "Courage is resistance to fear, mastery of fear—not absence of fear." —Mark Twain

Using Type 6 Arrow Lines for Growth

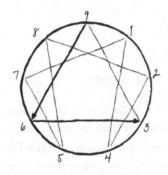

The two personality types connected to Type 6 by the arrow lines within the Enneagram diagram are Types 9 and 3. By focusing on embodying the healthy Type 9 ability to slow down and connect with people, then integrating Type 3's capacity for taking action, you can initiate a big growth shift from your usual focus on danger and risks, and concentrate on expanding your ability to do things before you feel 100 percent prepared.

- First, consciously adopt Type 9's ability to release tension by slowing down and connecting more with the people around you. Listen to others more deeply and allow yourself to trust their intentions. Play the role of the most easygoing person in the room to see how it feels. Dedicate time to activities that let you just "be." Get more grounded in your body and build up its strength. Allow your heart to calm down by sensing that your belly supports it. Feel your emotions through your body as a way of feeling more grounded and whole. Move out of your head, go with the flow, and blend with others' agendas without questioning anything.

- Then draw on Type 3's capacity for action without procrastination. Make a list of goals for yourself and focus on getting the results you want. Own more of your own effectiveness and competence. Do more self-promotion and let yourself be recognized for your positive qualities and accomplishments. Think about what will make you look good, not just how you can solve potential problems. Practice letting go of your fears about success and "just do it!" Get more in touch with your emotions and feel enthusiasm about moving forward instead of staying stuck in fear.

. . . .

"Success is not final, failure is not fatal: it is the courage to
continue that counts." —Winston Churchill

. . . .

EMBRACING THE HIGH SIDE

On the third part of their journey, this type realizes they can learn to be calm and confident and still make things happen in a positive way. They discover—much to their surprise—that they can feel strong inside without worrying and that the world won't fall apart. This feeling of strength comes from getting out of their heads and more into their hearts and bodies. When 6s learn to tap into the wisdom of their emotions and their gut as a way to balance out all the activity they generate in their heads, they find more ways to interrupt their thinking patterns that are fueled by doubt and anxiety. They learn that they have absolutely nothing to be afraid of and that they can let go of the control they thought they needed over potential threats and dangers. They learn to trust that everything will work out well. And when something doesn't work out, they can find the wisdom in that without immediately worrying about what will happen next.

If you identify as a Type 6, here are some things you can do on this part of your journey that you couldn't have done before—and what you can continue to work on:

- Counter fear with a natural sense of faith.

- Trust others more without as much testing and doubting. Trust yourself and own your abilities more easily and automatically.

- Stop over-thinking things so much and mapping out future scenarios all the time.

- Discern the difference between intuition and projection—when you are relaxed and correctly envisioning what's about to happen, as opposed to when you are tense and imagining that something bad is about to happen (that isn't actually happening).

- Exit negative thought loops by consulting your feelings and your gut.

- Flow with life with more lightness, spontaneity, and ease, without worrying about what will happen in the future.

- Experience more of an ability to calm yourself and be happier.

- Feel your own strength, power, and authority and develop the confidence to make decisions more easily, take action when you need to, and feel better about yourself generally.

- Focus on opportunities as much as you do on threats.

"One of the greatest discoveries a man makes, one of his great surprises, is to find he can do what he was afraid he couldn't do." —Henry Ford

The Type 6 Virtue

Courage is the virtue that provides an antidote to the Type 6 passion of fear. Through courage, 6s keep their hearts open in the face of anything that is happening (or may happen), and calmly but decisively take their next steps forward. They keep moving ahead because of a higher need or will, without any need to engage in a "fight-or-flight" response. They have a deep sense of confidence in their capacity to handle any challenge that comes their way. They trust themselves and the world, and don't need to imagine all the pitfalls they could experience before they forge ahead. They take full responsibility for their own lives, knowing they can deal with whatever life brings them.

Courage is the opposite of fear—a tendency to keep the heart open to whatever life may bring. Being courageous means moving forward despite unpredictability and taking action even when afraid. Courage provides this type with a healthy way of coping with fear by offering them a new and clear way forward. When they learn that they are really brave, their anxiety becomes pure energy. They remember episodes when the worst happened and they met the moment with a great deal of forcefulness and resilience. They remember when they maintained their composure in a crisis. And they understand that, in these moments, they exhibited at least some hints of the courage that they can now evoke in a conscious way regardless of what is happening around them.

If you are a Type 6, you can learn the true depth of your courage by working against your tendencies that are fueled by fear. Here are some courageous actions you can take to help you own your strength and live more from your full heart:

- Cease your mind's activity and "just do it" now—no time like the present.

- When you feel fear, go ahead anyway, without letting it hold you back. You can have your fear, just don't let it stop you.

- Find security within yourself—within your own body—free of contractions that come from anxiety.

- Pay attention to your inner reality and remain rooted in the present moment without replaying past hurts.

- Take in positive feedback from people who affirm your strength and stability.

- Reclaim your inner power and authority.

- Adopt a meditation practice to learn how to let go of problematic fear-based thoughts.

- Talk through your anxieties in a therapeutic setting as a way of facing them and getting (evidence-based) reality checks. Then let them go.

- Take on specific new challenges from a position of strength, trust, and confidence. Notice (and remember) when things turn out well because you applied your own power and strength to the situation.

"Scared is what you are feeling. Brave is what you're doing."
—Emma Donoghue

Waking Up from the Zombie State

For Type 6, the key to embracing the true self lies in quieting the mind. When this type clearly sees all the ways that their imaginations create problems that don't exist, they interrupt these thinking patterns and rest in a deeper sense of being secure inside themselves. When they regularly notice and let go of their focus on risks and problems, they allow themselves to open up to the possibility of a life beyond fear. This may seem very difficult when the ego tells them that the only way to be safe is to think of everything that can go wrong. But when they face and rise above their limiting beliefs, they empower their calm and grounded inner witness and achieve a higher degree of inner strength—one based firmly in self-knowledge and self-confidence. They gain a wider vision of who they are.

When 6s realize that getting stuck in suspicion and preparation prevents them from experiencing a peaceful sense of courage, they learn to focus all their intention and attention on relaxing into their true strength. When they regularly see through the empty threats caused by their negative thoughts, they begin to focus more on what's possible, firm in the faith that they have all the power they need to assure the best outcomes. By soothing themselves and trusting in their capacities as they move ahead into the unknown, they realize their true potential and see how the universe actually conspires for their joy and success. When they own and exercise their true power, they completely transform their mood and their outlook and manifest all the things they can create in the world.

Although this type must face shadows and difficulties just as other types do, the later stages of the Type 6 journey of awakening can be happier and more peaceful than expected. They may experience a greater sense of liberation, perhaps because they no longer dwell in difficulty or need to escape from it. Type 6 survival strategies focus on looking for problems and inadvertently inflict suffering. In zombie mode, 6s can't stop thinking that they need to keep seeking out every hidden problem and threat. But when they wake up to the way this mindset keeps them locked into a low level of awareness, they come home to an experience of their true selves, enjoy the immense relief of being able to take down their defenses, and reclaim the energy they spent managing their fear and all the stress that entails.

This type often believes that caution equals wisdom. This false assumption reinforces the tenacious hold of their self-limiting patterns. But when they finally surrender and accept that they can't control everything, they are able to own their true power to be brave when facing everything that happens in life. When they stop worrying about what is going to happen, or what might happen, they rest in presence. They develop the capacity to live life as it comes, which is the birthright of the true self. And on those occasions when the problems they imagined really *do* happen, they meet them with their natural, inborn strength. When 6s learn to trust regardless of what is happening in the moment, they come to know their inherent courage more fully, as the doorway to experiencing faith and a higher realization of all they really are.

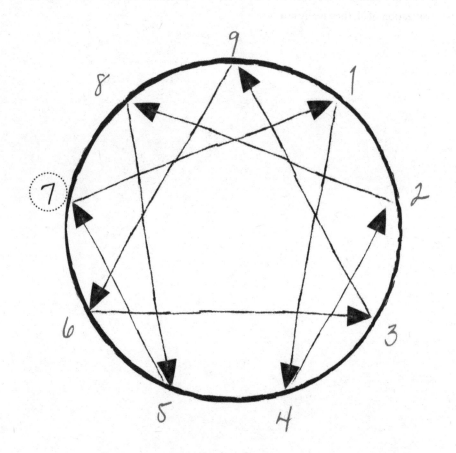

The Path from Gluttony to Sobriety

There is no path to happiness: Happiness is the path.

Buddha

O nce upon a time, there was a person named Seven. He was born with a natural sense of curiosity and wonder. He came into this world with a beautiful capacity for higher wisdom and true joy—a deep desire to focus intently on one thing at a time and to discover and take pleasure in each thing's essence. He loved concentrating all his attention on something he wanted to learn about and know deeply.

But one day, when Seven was paying close attention to a bee that was walking on his leg, it stung him! He burst into tears and looked around for someone to comfort him. He tried to tell his father about it and perhaps receive some comfort, but his father was angry about something and told him to "go away." So he went to his mother, but she was busy doing something and said she "didn't have time" to hear about something so insignificant. These responses made Seven feel even more pain—almost more than he could handle.

Seven hadn't had much experience with pain, and he didn't like it. So, to get away from these unpleasant sensations, he retreated into his own imagination. He started thinking about things that made him excited—watching clouds as they passed through the sky or playing with his best friend. In fact, Seven found that he was good at imagining fun and interesting things. As time went on, he became adept at diverting his attention to these thoughts whenever any kind of pain threatened him. Whenever he started feeling anything other than good or happy, he focused his attention on thinking about things that *felt* good or *seemed* happy.

Whenever he saw people who weren't happy, he wondered why they allowed that to happen. Why would anyone choose to feel bad when they could just think of something that made them feel good?

Over time, Seven developed an ability to make himself happy no matter what was going on around him. No matter what was happening in his life, he could always think of something that made him happy, or go to somewhere better in his mind to avoid sad or unhappy feelings. Then one day, his best friend moved away and, in a very small way, Seven began to feel the pain of losing him. But before that feeling could get very far into his awareness, he started thinking of all the other friends he would now have time to meet. He would just move on. Why wouldn't he? Thinking about his new fun future friends made him feel happy again. What Seven didn't realize, however, was that sometimes his happiness was superficial. Sometimes, it was just an escape and not true pleasure. It was not the pure joy he had felt when he was very young.

Seven didn't know that, sometimes, feeling pain can be important even if it doesn't feel "good." From his happy, pleasure-seeking perspective, he couldn't see that some emotional experiences can be rich and satisfying because they are real, even if they don't make us "happy." Sometimes we know real joy because we allow for the experience of pain. For Seven, it was true that he really loved his friend and he would really miss him. And feeling that pain was an opportunity for him to acknowledge that love—and the sadness that was also connected to that love.

But because Seven automatically avoided pain, without realizing it, he also avoided feeling his love. By avoiding his pain and insisting on feeling happy all the time, he eventually became unable to acknowledge many of his true feelings. He lost the ability to experience the true joy that comes with focusing deeply on one thing at a time—including all his feelings—and to take pleasure in whatever is real.

Seven had become a zombie—a very happy, fun-loving zombie, but a zombie just the same.

The Type 7 Checklist

If most or all of the following personality traits apply to you, you may be a Type 7:

☑ You focus much of your attention on interesting activities, stimulating ideas, and future possibilities.

☑ You actively look for ways to engage in pleasurable or fun experiences and worry about missing out on pleasure or fun.

☑ You avoid potentially uncomfortable situations by keeping your options open, finding opportunities for adventure, and maintaining your freedom.

☑ You habitually come up with positive ideas and plans that keep you focused on future possibilities.

☑ You value being free from limitations in life. You don't want to feel constrained by others or by situations.

☑ You seek to equalize authority and dislike hierarchies, because you don't like to be told what to do—or to tell others what to do.

☑ You are a highly optimistic person. You believe the future can always be bright.

☑ You have many interests and are a generalist—you specialize in not specializing.

☑ You have a difficult time facing pain and suffering in your life.

If you identify as a Type 7, your growth journey will follow three steps.

First, you will embark on the quest to know yourself by identifying the habitual patterns that keep you focused on what's positive to enable your (unconscious) avoidance of suffering.

Then you must face your Shadow by learning how your unconscious need to remain unaware of specific feelings and experiences makes you dependent on distractions and keeping your options open so you don't get trapped in bad situations or feelings.

Finally, you will discover how you can move toward the high side of your type by developing a capacity to receive everything that life brings you in any given moment and opening up to a deeper engagement with life, even when that entails feeling your pain.

"The most important thing is to enjoy your life—to be happy is all that matters." —Audrey Hepburn

EMBARKING ON THE QUEST

The first stage of the journey of awakening for Type 7s involves consciously recognizing how much attention they place on being happy, no matter what happens—without rationalizing and without judging themselves. By noticing how quickly their minds shift from one thing to another in an effort to maintain a positive mood, they begin to recognize that this effort to feel good all the time results in them not focusing on anything that might feel negative. This risks rendering their felt happiness superficial and ultimately unsatisfying.

Key Type 7 Patterns

As a Type 7, you may see no reason to question your relentless focus on staying positive. But your need to remain in a good mood may mask anxiety about being present to whatever's happening in the moment—or about having your freedom curtailed somehow. You may be seeking to escape from aspects of life you find boring or uncomfortable by distracting yourself from your "here-and-now" experience. And you may do this because you have an underlying fear of getting trapped in bad feelings from which you can't escape. The good news is that, if you can learn to tolerate more discomfort, the pain might not be as bad as you think—and it will make the good stuff more enjoyable by contrast.

If you identify as a Type 7, you can launch your growth journey by focusing on and making more conscious these five habitual patterns.

Needing Multiple Options

You may notice that you have a need to have many options (or courses of action) open to you. It will be important for you to observe yourself to see if you tend to move from one option to another if the first does not work out for some reason. You may notice that you tend to handle situations that might become uncomfortable or less-than-optimal by moving to another option at the last minute. You likely avoid feeling limited by anything in life, perhaps out of a sense of fear you may not fully acknowledge or be aware of. You tend to charm those you perceive might try to limit you in some way, thereby disarming them.

Focusing on Pleasure

You tend to want to indulge in pleasure or prioritize doing things you believe will make you feel happy, sometimes with negative consequences you may not acknowledge. Your focus on fun and pleasure may be fueled by a fear of getting trapped in a painful experience that never ends. Although you may not realize it, your focus on engaging in pleasurable experiences may mask a hidden desire (related to this fear) to avoid anything that feels painful. You may idealize some experiences and devalue others as a way of justifying the choices you make to experience more of what feels good and less of what doesn't feel good.

Rationalizing Your Focus on the Positive

It will help you to notice if you specialize in telling yourself stories to support what you want to do and think about. You likely always have good reasons to support anything you want to do for yourself. You may automatically create reasonable explanations for why your priorities (and indulgences) are good. You reinforce the wisdom of focusing only on the positive by denying that there might be any point to suffering or feeling bad. This tendency to find good reasons to validate or excuse anything you might want to do, think, or feel is best described as *rationalization*. For 7s, rationalization operates as a defensive mechanism to justify choices that put you, your pleasure, your positive outlook, and your plans ahead of anything else.

Avoiding Pain

Ask yourself if you build a life script based on being happy. Notice if you automatically reframe negatives into positives—and if you tend to "look at the bright side" and put a positive spin on things. You may try to keep your mood up by focusing on whatever helps you to feel good and avoid feeling bad, perhaps as an unconscious strategy to avoid any kind of suffering. Observe yourself to see if you have trouble acknowledging any fear you have of pain, or if you find it hard to open up to feeling painful emotions. You may not see any reason why feeling pain would be a good idea. By avoiding bad feelings, however, you may tend to skim along the surface of life, instead of being more fully available to experience a deeper level of what's happening in the present moment.

Avoiding Difficult Situations

In much the same way that you may avoid pain without even thinking about it, you may also try to avoid dealing with difficult situations in life and relationships. We all face challenges and problems in relationships, and facing them often deepens and strengthens our connections with others. But it will be important for you to notice if you inadvertently keep your relationships at a superficial level because you don't want to confront what's not working. You may try to "slide and skate" when it comes to working through rough spots with others by being indirect and unclear—or avoiding things entirely. It will be important for you to observe yourself to see if you do this and if this tendency sometimes causes you problems.

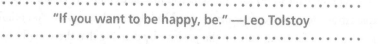

"If you want to be happy, be." —Leo Tolstoy

The Type 7 Passion

Gluttony is the passion that drives Type 7. In its expression as the core emotional motivation of this type, gluttony fuels the desire to experience pleasure without limits, to taste a little bit of every experience, and to stay open to myriad possibilities.

Gluttony can be understood as a passion for variety, not just overindulgence in food and drink. It motivates this type to want to experience all the possibilities in life and avoid any constraints that might force them to experience less. They put a lot of effort into guaranteeing that they can indulge in many different kinds of pleasures and satisfy their immediate desires, including those connected to the mind. They usually have very busy, quick, and active minds that constantly and rapidly come up with new ideas and make plans in imaginative ways. But when this type seeks to grow, they must moderate their excessive need to seek entertainment for their minds. When 7s begin to see the drawbacks of gluttony, they can slow down and sink more deeply into one experience at a time.

This type runs the risk of being distracted from what really matters in life. For instance, they may sometimes decide to experience something new at the cost of achieving a more promising result by sticking with an old (perhaps more mundane) experience. They may prioritize having several different kinds of work experiences rather than specializing in one area. When they get good at something, they sometimes feel the urge to move on to something else because they don't want to feel bored. It can be hard for them to stay with one thing, and they can become restless unless they have access to a wide variety of experiences.

If you are a Type 7, you must observe and make conscious these typical manifestations of gluttony to move forward on your path to awakening:

- Trying not to miss out on any possibilities or opportunities.

- Engaging in multiple interests at a time, multitasking, or jumping from one activity to another.

- Putting a positive spin on things, reframing negatives into positives, and avoiding whatever seems bad or boring.

- Getting easily distracted by whatever looks new and interesting or exciting—the "bright shiny object" syndrome.

- Talking about multiple themes at once and changing subjects quickly.

- Feeling amazed, fascinated, thrilled, energized, or excited.

- Experiencing a sense of urgency to pursue pleasure or a specific adventure, or to switch course to something more pleasurable or fun.

- Making mental connections and associations between different things. Thinking "outside the box."

- Losing focus on the here and now by imagining plans for the future. Not finishing what you started.

. . . .

"Curiousity is gluttony. To see is to devour."
—Victor Hugo

. . . .

Using Type 7 Wings as Growth Stretches

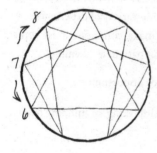

The two personality types adjacent to Type 7 on the Enneagram circle are Types 6 and 8. By leaning into the Type 6 ability to perceive and address what's not ideal, and then integrating the Type 8 capacity to commit to a bold course of action, this type can move beyond their habitual patterns related to being easily distracted and overly optimistic.

- First, adopt Type 6's tendency to pay more attention to the risks you run when you don't follow through on implementing plans or projects, or double-check all the details. Get in touch with any fears or concerns that will help you ensure that everything you do gets done well. Consider whether you engage in relationships in superficial ways and deepen your commitments based on really feeling a desire to be responsible and demonstrate loyalty. Face difficult conversations you may need to have and commit to fixing any problems you have avoided addressing. Take responsibility for assuring that problems get solved.

- Then integrate Type 8's ability to make clearer decisions about what to prioritize. Stop participating in activities that don't really add anything meaningful to your life or that don't advance your progress toward your goals. Look at existing challenges that need to be met, rather than new opportunities to explore. Take action to solve problems in a direct way, even when it proves difficult. Be practical and finish things you need to finish. Act to implement one or two good ideas rather than generating many. Do the most important thing first, not the thing you like the most. Be clear, direct, decisive, and assertive in your communication. Practice taking charge and moving straight ahead rather than getting distracted.

. . . .

"No one escapes pain, fear and suffering."
—Eric Greitens

. . . .

FACING THE SHADOW

The second part of the Type 7 growth journey is all about acknowledging, accepting, and integrating the tendency to avoid what feels bad by focusing on what feels good. By learning that true pleasure comes only through being open to pain, 7s grow as they begin to make what's unconscious conscious and realize that their tendency to focus on what's positive (which they thought was a good thing) can be a bad thing. When this type lacks this self-awareness, they succumb to a need to avoid looking at things that can be difficult. But their need to evade suffering must be faced and made more conscious if they want to emerge from their zombie state.

When Type 7s ignore negative data or uncomfortable emotions, they may become blind to the value of engaging more deeply with difficult feelings and situations. When this happens, they may miss out on the richness of some experiences that may seem challenging and can become stuck in living very superficial lives. When what seems to be happening in the present doesn't fulfill their idealized expectations, they can become disappointed or even depressed. This part of their path requires that they develop the ability to face things that are hard to feel or admit, and find more mature solutions to persistent problems they may have typically wanted to sidestep. This can be particularly hard for them, because it means facing their fear of suffering in order to live life with more depth and courage.

Meeting the Type 7 Shadow

If you identify as a Type 7, here are some actions you can take to bring to the surface, become more aware of, and start working to counteract the key unconscious patterns, blind spots, and pain points of the type:

- Look at your cravings to see what triggers them. While everyone needs to experience pleasure, being dependent on feeling good may fuel addictive behavior that stems from unacknowledged fear or sadness.

- Observe how engaging people with stories and other forms of intellectual seduction may help you rationalize problems, deflect discomfort, or maintain freedom.

- Examine whether your style of charming and disarming people who might have problems with you may work sometimes, but may also deepen discord in the long run.

- Confront your "inner pessimist." Although you appear optimistic, you need to see and own the part of you that believes that, if you don't relentlessly stay positive ("look on the bright side"), you will be trapped in a bad feeling forever.

- Notice whether your belief that your pain won't go away if you allow yourself to feel it is limiting you without you realizing it.

- Ask yourself if, when you become uninterested in something, the quality of what you do goes down.

- Recognize how keeping your options open until the last minute leads to letting people down when you abruptly back out of commitments and promises.

- Own that your drive for instant gratification may come from anxiety related to facing pain or limitation.

- Examine your tendency to be self-referencing—to put your attention primarily on what you want and need. Notice how this can lead to a lack of empathy or support for others.

· ·

"From pain can come wisdom, from fear can come courage,
from suffering can come strength—if we have
the virtue of resilience." —Eric Greitens

· ·

The Type 7 Blind Spots

Type 7s may not want to examine their blind spots because they habitually avoid engaging with experiences connected to painful emotions or anything that seems negative. Their main survival strategy leads them automatically to find escape routes when it comes to uncomfortable feelings. However, it will be important for them to become aware of any feelings like insecurity or anxiety that they may regularly experience beneath their happy exterior. They tend to resist looking at what has the potential to bring on fear or sadness by focusing on positive opportunities and the brighter side of things. And they may hide that avoidance (and any anxiety they may feel that fuels it) behind a carefree image of self-confidence. Further, their gluttony may drive a hunger for feeling only pleasurable experiences, which can block their growth without them realizing it.

But here's some good news if you identify with this type. If you are willing to look at your blind spots and feel any pain that arises, it will get easier to handle your deeper feelings with a new sense of maturity. This type can resemble the archetype of the "eternal child" and resist growing up in different ways. So, if you are a 7, it will be important for you to remember that, if you develop confidence and resilience in the face of pain, you will be rewarded. And you will not lose the capacity for having fun and enjoying life as you fear you may. Any pain you consciously choose to feel will pass away after it brings you the information it has to share with you.

Here are some of the habitual patterns that operate as blind spots that you, as a Type 7, need to make more conscious in order to move forward on your path.

Avoiding Problems

Do you find something else to focus on when you face challenges? When you do acknowledge that problems exist, do you tend to run away, distract yourself, or devise a quick fix? Here are some things you can do to integrate this blind spot:

- Allocate some time every day to work on problematic issues, no matter how it feels. Make sure you do all you need to do. When you finish, do something fun, so that your ego allows you to do this again.

- With a psychotherapist or close friend you trust, talk about all the ways you have been distracting yourself from problems throughout your life. Notice if you resist being fully honest, make excuses, or whitewash things.

- Notice when you distract yourself from facing something difficult or something you label as "boring" and ask yourself why. What do you fear will happen if you deal with the issue? How will you benefit from dealing with it now? What good things will you feel after having dealt with it?

- Become aware of any thoughts or feelings that convince you your problems look worse than they actually are. On the other hand, do you persist in claiming that your problems don't exist?

- Admit that you need help to focus on specific difficult issues and ask people to coach you through dealing with these problems.

- Reflect more deeply on the emotions you avoid when you evade challenging situations.

Avoiding Accountability

Do you rationalize to avoid problems as a way of denying responsibility for them? Do you create a false version of the facts to hide flaws you fear you may have? Here are some things you can do to integrate this blind spot:

- Recognize your underlying motives every time you try to minimize your responsibility by making something relative or somehow "not so bad."

- Become aware of the positive story you try to defend when you don't hold yourself accountable. Ask yourself if it masks an unacknowledged fear of failure.

- Acknowledge the hard time you have facing some of your adult responsibilities because they seem tedious or boring or limiting. You may have a bit of a "Peter Pan" complex that makes you play the role of the "eternal child."

- Be aware of any desire to share responsibility with others more than (perhaps) is warranted.

- Ask others to point out when you rationalize—or find good reasons—to avoid accountability. Notice and tolerate the feelings that arise when they help you to face reality.

- Admit to yourself and to someone you trust that you have a natural tendency to run away from taking full responsibility for things that don't work out well. When you succeed in holding yourself accountable, notice how this can also feel good.

Disregarding Pain and Negative Data

Do you focus on what feels good to avoid what might feel bad? Do you pursue what feels pleasant without realizing you are also avoiding something? Do you automatically reframe negatives as positives? Do you sometimes just "not see" the negatives of a situation? Here are some actions you can take to integrate this blind spot:

- Notice how hard it is to look at and talk about anything that seems negative. What stands in your way of accepting what's true when it doesn't feel good?

- Become more aware of how focusing only on good feelings acts as a defense against experiencing painful feelings. Think deeply about all the reasons you distract yourself from any kind of difficult emotions.

- Notice any situations in your life that have worsened as a result of your resistance to acknowledging fear, anxiety, sadness, or pain. Own that your dislike of anything you identify as "boring" or uncomfortable operates as a way to avoid negative emotions.

- Observe your tendency to see only the good side of things. Notice if you do this even more if you sense that some negative data exists somewhere.

- Explore your tendency to focus on how to improve things without truly facing what isn't working.

- Recognize when you find it difficult to feel disappointed when situations don't turn out the way you wanted them to—and then consciously allow yourself to feel the disappointment.

"Rationalization is allowing my mind to find a reason to excuse what my spirit knows is wrong." —Bruce Eamon Brown

Type 7 Pain

Psychology and spiritual teachings tell us that, when we seek only pleasure in life, we often end up feeling unsatisfied (or worse). Getting in touch with pain often means we can feel more joy, because pain and joy can be seen as two sides of the same coin. When we avoid negative emotions, we tend to dampen our positive feelings as well. But we all need to face our pain with an open heart to achieve wholeness, because our emotions reflect important aspects of who we are and give us information about what is true for us.

When Type 7s decide to face their pain, they take important steps toward becoming more grounded, more peaceful, and more truly happy—not just nervously or superficially happy. They can do this by acknowledging two key needs: the need to ask for support and the need to take the time required, trusting that the pain won't last forever.

If you identify with this type, remember that we all experience pain. When you allow yourself to feel your pain, you feel better for having learned to tolerate it. And, even better, you stop creating more pain for yourself through avoiding your pain. To accelerate your healing and growth, slowly learn to experience these specific painful feelings:

- An underlying anxiety about getting trapped in an unpleasant emotional experience from which you can't escape. You are a good escape artist; you excel at deflecting attention from discomfort and negative emotions, and focusing on good feelings. But if you can face this fear, it makes all the other painful feelings on this list easier to handle and less scary.

- Fear about being limited. It will be good for you to acknowledge your need to maintain control over your freedom and the fact that you dislike being told what to do. You probably don't like having your ability to do what you want to do limited in any way. Notice and feel any fear of being constrained—and see what you do to avoid this.

- Fear of "negative" experiences. You may not have much capacity for empathy because you tend to avoid your own pain. You may also tend to be self-referencing, meaning you pay more attention to your own inner experience than to that of others. If others try to share their pain or sadness with you, you may just tell them to "look on the bright side," because it's hard for you to sit still with pain. By opening up to your own difficult emotions, however, you can begin to experience richer connections with others.

- Pain and your fear of being overwhelmed by it. You must open up to pain or you risk becoming addicted to the things you do to avoid it—ingesting substances, working too hard, or taking refuge in superficial distractions. Reframe pain as part of the intrinsic fullness of life. When you become conscious of your pain, you open yourself to the wonderful experiences that only occur when you welcome pain—being truly close to others, stepping fully into the unknown to experience new things, and being fully present and available in the moment.

- The sadness you may feel because you may not allow yourself to feel emotions that are naturally part of life. At some point, however, these feelings will probably emerge—sometimes as sadness at not having been able to feel emotion and pain before. If this happens, let yourself feel them, even if it feels scary. Find a friend or therapist to support you and remind you that the pain of sadness won't last forever. But be with your sadness for a little while to see what it has to teach you about yourself.

· ·

"Invite suffering in, so that it can go away."
—Sufi saying

· ·

The Type 7 Subtypes

Identifying your Type 7 subtype can help you target your efforts to confront your blind spots, unconscious tendencies, and hidden pain. The specific patterns and tendencies of the subtypes vary depending on which of the three survival instincts dominates your experience.

Self-Preservation 7 Subtype

This subtype is pragmatic and excels at making alliances. They create a family-like network through which they can get their needs met. They tend to be alert and open to opportunities for pleasure and for making a good deal. They are cheerful, talkative, and hedonistic. They are the most self-referencing subtype and their empathy tends to be the most underdeveloped.

Social 7 Subtype

This subtype cares about others and sacrifices for other people in selfless ways, as they tend to want to be careful not to exploit opportunities for their own advantage. Their gluttony gets directed toward a wish to be good and pure, and so they often focus on doing some kind of work aimed at reducing suffering in the world. They are drawn to professions in which they alleviate pain. They pay attention to the larger collective and tend to hold a Utopian vision of the world—they express enthusiasm for envisioning a better world.

Sexual (One-to-One) 7 Subtype

This subtype is idealistic and dreams of a better world. They may have trouble being in touch with ordinary reality as they live more from their imagination of how they would like things to be. They tend to be very happy and excessively enthusiastic—they see the world as better than it actually is. They have a tendency to fantasize and be somewhat naive, perceiving the world through "rose-colored glasses." They have a tendency to be fascinated with ideas and people. They may seem gullible and susceptible to other people's opinions, interests, and energy.

The Type 7 Subtype Shadows

You can more effectively confront your Shadow if you know the specific shadow characteristics of your subtype. Below are some of the shadow aspects of each subtype. As subtype behavior can be highly automatic and unconscious, these traits can be the hardest to see and own.

Self-Preservation 7 Shadow

If this is your subtype, you will need to observe yourself to see if you take opportunistic stances and sometimes take advantage of people. You may tend to use others for your own benefit, or disregard their needs and feelings. As you tend to be very self-referencing and self-interested, this can lead you to put yourself first in a way that you may not own and that can be selfish. You may value your head more than your heart much of the time, and may not be very in touch with your emotions or very sensitive to the emotions of others. To grow, you will need to become more aware of how much you act from self-interest.

Social 7 Shadow

If this is your subtype, you tend to present yourself as a good, humble, and self-sacrificing person, but this can hide an unconscious superiority complex that makes you feel better (and more unselfish) than others. You dedicate yourself to causes that address others' pain, but this may actually serve your need to avoid your own unacknowledged pain while proving your goodness. You help others in exaggerated ways, but this may not always be completely altruistic. It may also be motivated by your intolerance of pain generally and your need to be good—or to be seen as good (and not selfish or self-interested). You need to learn to be less available to help others, to address your own needs and desires, and to go against your taboo on selfishness.

Sexual (One-to-One) 7 Shadow

If this is your subtype, your idealism, enthusiasm, and optimism may lead you to disconnect from reality in ways you don't see. You may be blind to things you do that don't serve you (or others). Your creativity may come with a tendency to fantasize, which can lead to being excessively positive. You tend to display the most intolerance for dealing with pain and negative data. Your gluttony for seeing the positive in everything may mean that other people easily influence you. You may tend to avoid dealing with reality in ways that cause real harm.

> "The most painful thing is losing yourself in the process
> of loving someone too much, and forgetting that
> you are special too." —Ernest Hemingway

The Type 7 Paradox

The Type 7 paradox arises from the polarity between the passion of gluttony and the virtue of sobriety. Sobriety is the heart's capacity for feeling a sense of satisfaction in focusing on one important thing. For this type, recognizing the things they have missed in their lives because of their gluttonous attachment to pleasure and diversity allows them to become more aware of a central aspect of their passion—the tendency to skim along the surface of life and avoid a deeper engagement with their life exprience. By becoming more aware of how gluttony operates, they learn to say "no" to lesser priorities and focus on one thing at a time. They develop the capacity to be more present and still.

If you identify with this type, here are some first steps you can take toward becoming more conscious of your gluttony and accessing the higher-level state of sobriety:

- Notice when you get anxious and want to stop an activity you judge as "boring." Take some conscious breaths, sense your body, and calm your heart. If you stay present, your experience will be neutral, not boring.

- When you get excited about something "amazing," try to balance enthusiasm with stillness. Excitement triggers or results from gluttony.

- Identify activities that help you concentrate. Do more of whatever helps you focus and less of whatever leads you to distract yourself.

- Gradually stop overstimulating yourself with movement, sound, imagination, and other experiences that lead you to speed up and disperse your focus. For you, less is more.

- Make conscious efforts to recall moments in your life that have been hard. Stay in touch with them for longer periods of time, without redefining them as easier or lighter than they actually were.

- List all the activities and plans that remain unfinished in your life. Courageously decide to complete one of these today or in the next week.

Using Type 7 Arrow Lines for Growth

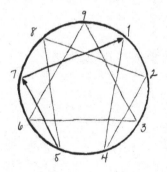

The two personality types connected to Type 7 by the internal arrow lines within the Enneagram diagram are Types 5 and 1. By intentionally embodying Type 5's ability to go inside, stay more internal, and dive deeper into one action, and then integrating Type 1's capacity to be grounded and disciplined, you can create two different kinds of radical shifts that will help you move out of your habitual focus on generating ideas, multitasking, and thinking of future plans and possibilities.

- First, adopt Type 5's practice of paying more attention to whatever happens inside you. Balance your tendency to innovate with a focus on learning about something in greater depth. Counteract your focus on what's exciting out there in the world by paying more attention to your own inner processes. Practice staying more inside yourself and becoming quieter and more calm. Learn to enjoy concentrating on one specific thing at a time. Specialize in something rather than being a "jack of all trades and master of none." Develop more consistency, thoughtfulness, and objectivity in what you do.

- Then work to integrate Type 1's ability to be more grounded in the body in the present moment. Enjoy a new capacity to stay focused on one important priority. Be more intentional and selective about what needs to be done, instead of being carried along with the excitement of the moment. Focus on fewer projects and follow through on them to the end. Enhance your ability to concentrate and your sense of responsibility. Focus on delivering things on time with a high level of quality. Develop your ability to be more practical and process-oriented when it comes to implementing your ideas.

. . . .

"If you want to make God laugh, tell him your plans."
—Sufi saying

. . . .

Embracing the High Side

On the third part of their journey, 7s remember the peace and beauty of staying present to what life brings them. They learn to be fully available for what they are experiencing right now. They welcome whatever comes, without judging it as good or bad, and stop resisting the inherent wisdom of life by needing to impose their own plans to ensure their freedom. In fact, when 7s do the work to get to this stage of their growth path, they see that life works in magical ways to bring us our most important opportunities for growth, even when this means facing challenges and difficulties. When they grow beyond their zombie mode, this type sees the challenges that arise in life as learning opportunities that can lead to a deeper kind of joy and fulfillment that is sometimes hard-won.

Type 7s who wake up and begin to remember who they really are reduce their usual fast pace and start moving through life more slowly. They stop making so many plans and no longer feel the need to escape into their minds and into the future. They learn to feel less excited about things they previously considered fantastic—and less discouraged about things they formerly perceived as horrible. They still exhibit the creativity and innovative thinking that comes naturally to them, but they don't have to skip so quickly from one thing to another or charm people to avoid any experience of limitation. They understand the wisdom of taking things as they come and feel more neutral and stable in experiencing the present moment. They are no longer limited by their fear of being bored and know they can find pleasure and satisfaction in every moment, even if nothing particularly fascinating happens.

At this stage on their journey, this type becomes capable of existing peacefully in a state of calm, focused, relaxed joy. They feel amazed by being in touch not only with their now more quiet minds but also with their hearts and the feelings they need no longer fear. They find deep satisfaction in sensing that their bodies are more connected to the earth. They may still keep their heads in the sky to dream and imagine, but they also keep their feet on the ground and stay more closely attuned to reality. This helps them put their ideas into action.

If you identify as a Type 7, here are some things you can do at this stage of your journey that you couldn't have done before—and what you can continue to work on:

- Focus on the one priority that will make the biggest difference and be happy about it.

- Pay less attention to things you may be missing and value your present encounters more.

- Let go of your "monkey mind" and feel more balanced and relaxed.

- Finish projects and appreciate the benefits of completion and fulfillment.

- Be less anxious about imagining all the possibilities and pleasures in life and enjoy one experience at a time more fully—all the way through to the end.

- Build better relationships by having greater empathy for others.

- Welcome all your emotions without fear, knowing they are just passing through. Feel your emotions all the way through to completion, confident in your ability to experience them and move through them.

- Balance the good with the bad, and acknowledge what they both have to teach you.

. . . .
**"Life is what happens when you are busy
making other plans." —Allen Sounders**
. . . .

The Type 7 Virtue

Sobriety is the virtue that provides an antidote to Type 7 gluttony. Sobriety opposes gluttony as the heart's capacity to feel a deep sense of satisfaction in focusing on one important thing at a time. Sobriety helps this type appreciate sticking with an experience all the way through to the end. In this context, it means reducing excess movement and coming to stillness. In sobriety, this type becomes more committed to things and people and rejects their exaggerated need for mental stimulation and distractions. They feel more serious and less relentlessly happy—but still happy enough. Sobriety offers this type a clear goal to work toward after consciously observing their gluttony and the patterns that flow from it.

If you are a Type 7, here are some steps you can take to move you forward on your path toward a greater realization of the virtue of sobriety:

- Stay present to one thing at a time.

- Adopt a meditation practice.

- Open your heart to whatever emotions arise. Address suffering by engaging with it rather than escaping from it.

- Become more strongly rooted in your body and less anxiously active.

- Hold a mature perspective; know it pays to postpone short-term gratification for the sake of fulfilling meaningful commitments.

- Orient yourself to the deeper truth of lived experience rather than just the pursuit of enjoyment.

- Let go of "the pleasure principle" in favor of what brings real satisfaction in the long term.

- Talk less and do fewer things that distract you and others from being present.

- Exchange your desires for needs that are more real, relevant, and long-lasting.

- Operate from a sense of reason, emotional steadiness, and grounded self-confidence, rather than being swept away by impulses and fantasies.

. . . .

"Focus and simplicity: once you get there,
you can move mountains." —Steve Jobs

. . . .

Waking Up from the Zombie State

For Type 7s, the key to embracing the true self lies in being in touch with reality as it is and not as they wish or imagine it to be. In a world with so many problems and so much pain, this can seem difficult, as our egos tell us we can feel better if we make things look more positive than they are. But when this type faces their blind spots and owns their pain, they can rise above their impulsive need to avoid any kind of discomfort or limitation and live from a higher degree of self-knowledge and self-respect that flows from a wider vision of who they can be and what they can feel.

When this type begins having more satisfying, more reality-based experiences and stops living from an imagined sense of life as they would like it to be, they feel more alive than ever. They experience a wonderful sense of deep integrity, rather than just superficial levity. They live in the here and now, rather than being lost in thoughts, dreams, distractions, and fantasies. This is an arduous task for them at first. At times, they may fear that life means dwelling forever in pain. But when they really commit to their own inner work, they realize it's worth it—*they* are worth it. They discover unexpected rewards—like more balance, more presence, and a different kind of pleasure. They reconnect to their hearts and their souls and are rewarded with true joy and the deepest kind of pleasure. They experience the richness of being fully present to their experience and fully appreciate the exciting adventure of being in reality and taking life as it comes.

When this type awakens from their "happy zombie" state, they experience states of being that they never imagined possible and become deeply grounded and capable of intense focused concentration. They develop the ability to enjoy one thing at a time, while maintaining their focus and commitment to the end. As they become more serious and responsible, they feel better and better—much to their surprise—and derive deep satisfaction from everything they experience. When they learn to tell the difference between everyday happiness and true joy, they find fulfillment in both joy and pain, and in everything else that life brings them.

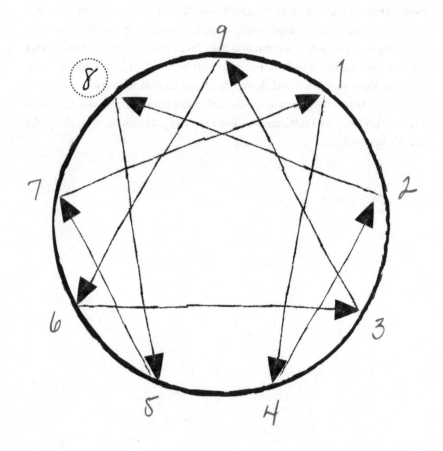

Type 8

The Path from Lust to Innocence

If you are patient in one moment of anger,
you will escape a hundred days of sorrow.

<small>CHINESE PROVERB</small>

Once upon a time, there was a person named Eight. She came into this world as a sensitive and sweet child. She was completely innocent, as all children are. She had a lot of energy, always saw the best in people, and was eager to learn all she could about the world.

But early in life, Eight had an experience in which she needed protection and there was no one there to take care of her. Sometimes there were things she just couldn't do by herself, even though she was bright and capable for someone so young. The people in her life that were bigger than she was didn't seem to notice when she needed to be cared for, listened to, or fed. And a few times, when one of the older kids hurt her, no one saw that she was little and needed protection.

So Eight learned—the hard way—that she had to take care of herself. If no one else was going to do it, it would have to be her job. She would have to get big—fast! (Too fast.) She would have to be strong. She would have to be powerful, even though she was still small. Sometimes people around her fought, and they didn't notice she was scared. So she would have to be fearless, in addition to being big, and strong, and powerful.

Eight had a lot of natural energy, so in time she became fully able to protect herself. She became strong and learned how to take care of herself by herself—and sometimes other people as well. She learned to be scary instead of being scared. And she was good at it! One thing that helped her to be as strong as she needed to be was her ability to get angry. Sometimes, when someone did something she didn't like, she could get very angry very quickly. Anger felt like energy rushing through her body and, although she didn't always plan to get angry (or even want to), it helped her a lot. Her anger helped her to be even more fearless—and even more scary. And appearing large, angry, and scary made it possible for her to feel fully capable of taking care of herself.

Eventually, Eight didn't even notice when she wasn't protected by the people from whom she expected protection, because she didn't feel so helpless any more. The only problem was that now *many* things made her angry. And, in a way, she liked being angry—or at least didn't mind it. It just happened, especially when she needed someone and there was no one there for her, or when older girls bullied her at school because they sensed her power and didn't like it.

Soon, Eight didn't even notice when no one supported her, because she could support herself so well. She didn't need anyone. She was strong enough. And everyone else seemed much weaker than she was. She was told that sometimes she scared people even when she wasn't trying to. Sometimes people left when she entered a room or stopped talking after she spoke loudly. She wasn't sure what was wrong with them. Why weren't others as strong as she was? Weak people made her angry, and her anger made her feel strong and full of energy. But sometimes she saw that weak people were treated badly or unfairly, and then she used her strength to help them if they needed it.

Every once in a while, Eight felt a little bit lonely. She discovered that sometimes, when she was the most powerful person around, others didn't want to be close to her. She didn't really understand it, but that's the way it was. And she was mostly okay with that, because she could usually get what she wanted. All she had to do was become angry and scare a few people. She didn't really care if anyone liked her. She had lost the sensitivity she was born with. It didn't really work to be sensitive *and* strong and powerful, and she needed to be powerful to take care of herself.

Soon Eight noticed that she couldn't stop getting angry; she couldn't stop being strong and powerful. And why should she? She wasn't sensitive and innocent anymore. Being that way reminded her too much of when she was too small and weak to protect herself. It was much better to be strong and powerful. She always knew how to take care of everything. Why would she give that up to feel like a scared little girl again? Occasionally, she felt a little bit alone because almost no one was as strong as she was. She sometimes got a tiny bit sad because there was never anyone there to take care of her. She had to take care of everyone. But then she would sense her own energy and strength, and she would feel glad that she was so powerful. Nothing and no one could hurt her. That seemed like a good thing, even though it was sometimes hard on her.

Eight had become a zombie—a forceful, unstoppable, unapproachable zombie, but a zombie just the same.

The Type 8 Checklist

If most or all of the following personality traits apply to you, you may be a Type 8:

☑ You usually come across as assertive and direct.

☑ You specialize in taking action quickly and decisively—and sometimes impulsively.

☑ You focus much of your attention on working to ensure justice or fairness and try to bring truth and order to everything you do.

☑ You have a difficult time containing your reactions when you feel angry.

☑ You value honesty, directness, and authenticity. You tell the truth and want others to do the same. With you, "what you see is what you get."

☑ You have a lot of energy and enjoy taking on big challenges; you don't back down when confronted with a difficult situation.

☑ While you may say you don't necessarily like conflict, you can engage in it when needed.

☑ You can sometimes be excessive in the things you do—for example, eating, drinking, or working too much.

☑ You tend to be protective of those you care about.

☑ You seek to express strength and power in the things you do and avoid appearing weak in any way.

If, after using this checklist, you identify as a Type 8, your growth journey will follow three steps.

First, you will embark on the quest to know yourself by learning to see more clearly how you depend on projecting strength and power to avoid vulnerability.

Then you must face your Shadow to become more aware of your fear of showing weakness. This will help you recognize the ways in which you need to be powerful and action-oriented in the things you do but also develop the ability to get in touch with basic human emotions like fear, sadness, and insecurity.

The final stage of your journey involves learning to acknowledge and fully experience your vulnerability and your natural sensitivity. This makes you softer, more open, and more approachable.

. . . .

Vulnerability is not weakness; it's our greatest measure
of courage." —Brené Brown

. . . .

EMBARKING ON THE QUEST

The first stage of awakening for this type involves noticing how they try to control things and impose their will on others. By mindfully observing this habitual pattern in action, 8s begin to recognize how much attention they place on asserting power in the world and restoring justice, sometimes even when it doesn't involve them directly. This gives them the sense that they can't let down their guard or express any kind of weakness. When they start to see this tendency as a consequence of feeling that they have to appear strong and protect themselves (and others), they take a step forward on the path to growth.

Key Type 8 Patterns

If you identify with this type, you can launch your growth journey by focusing on and making more conscious these five habitual Type 8 patterns.

Being in Charge

You probably have a history of assuming either formal or informal leadership roles in your professional and personal life without knowing exactly how or why. While you would likely say you don't always feel the need to be in charge, when you sense a power vacuum that needs to be filled, you readily step forward. This is because, as an 8, you have a natural talent for taking the lead. Your naturally assertive and courageous style leads you to gravitate toward being the boss—whether because others want you to be or because you want to make sure someone capable is in charge. You have a tendency to want to direct what's happening—and you can do this in either a skillful and confident way, or a bossy or pushy way.

Engaging in Conflict

Notice if you easily voice disagreement with others' opinions or actions. When you perceive incompetence, unfairness, or mistakes, you may have difficulty not saying or doing something. Observe yourself to see if you almost always want to address anything you see as problematic quickly, without necessarily waiting to choose the right words or approach. You likely have no problem initiating a conflict that may move things forward or redress an injustice. This tendency may lead you to rebel against established authority, or question or break rules. This may lead to others experiencing you as confrontational, difficult, or domineering. But it may also be your way of showing that you care. And it may reflect the fact that you have difficulty containing yourself when something feels important to you and you actually develop trust with others through going up against them in a conflict.

Taking Action to Address Unjust Situations Yourself

Observe yourself to see if you have a built-in radar for spotting unjust and unfair situations, or if you have a natural tendency to jump into action as soon as possible. You may have an implicit belief that you must be the one to deliver justice and right all the wrongs you see in the world. Consider if this reflects your need to express power in the world—both because you can't help being strong and because real injustices bother you. It will also be important for you to acknowledge if you have a tendency to "forget yourself" when you do this—automatically playing the superhero without seeing or acknowledging any negative impacts or threats this may hold for you.

Operating at a High Level of Intensity

It may be hard for you to be balanced, cautious, and discrete because of your natural tendency to act from impulse, to exaggerate, and to become excessive or unrestrained. You get intense when doing things or expressing yourself, and may have an "all or nothing" approach to life. Notice if moderation comes hard for you and you get more passionate or extreme than other people without understanding where this intensity comes from or what purpose it serves. Explore your relationship to intensity and ask yourself what life would bring if you were less intense.

Seeking Vengeance

Notice if you tend to think about what you will do in response to others' actions when you don't like them or find them hurtful, wrong, or unfair. Observe yourself to see if you sometimes become aggressive in direct proportion to how much you deny your own sensitivity as a way of getting back at people without being fully aware of the ways they may have hurt you. It will be important for you to understand that vengeance can take different forms, and to explore the possibility that you may not always know the difference between healthy anger and vengeful aggression. Explore why you may take action against those you think have done something wrong—even if you rationalize your actions as subtle or insignificant. Notice if you sometimes act from vengeance in less obvious, more long-term ways. Consider where this impulse comes from in you.

> "Lust is a poor, weak, whimpering, whispering thing compared with that richness and energy of desire which arises when lust has been killed." —C. S. Lewis

The Type 8 Passion

The passion that drives Type 8 is lust. As the core emotional motivation behind this type, lust is excess—a passion for excess in all types of stimulation. It especially implies seeking excessive fulfillment through the senses or physical experience, although it does not necessarily refer to anything sexual.

For 8s, lust also implies an impatience or urgency to have their desires satisfied. They don't like to wait or negotiate or feel limited. They tend to be impatient, imposing, and rebellious against anyone who tries to limit or control them. They usually resist any constraints around pleasure and the satisfaction of their physical, emotional, and intellectual appetites—whether for food, fun, sex, or even work. They describe themselves as "working hard and playing hard," and this reflects their lustful disposition. As an emotional coping strategy, they defy authority and make sure that they stay completely in charge of their own lives. But this can also compel them to put themselves too much in charge of others' lives.

This type can exhibit the excess of lust in a wide range of ways, including liking something or someone a lot, or not liking them at all. They may engage in a certain activity all the time, or not at all. They may speak in either a very loud or an extremely low voice; they may get almost no sleep or want to sleep all the time. Some of their excesses may seem "harmless"—like being *very* excited about something or becoming extremely calm or withdrawn once they discover and regret how aggressive they can be.

Lust also drives this type's tendency to be intense and their difficulty slowing down or working less. It also underlies their struggle to moderate their energy, intensity, or effort. It manifests in the forcefulness of their communication style and their tendency to act quickly and decisively without stopping to think first. They may do too much too fast, or not give themselves enough down time, denying that they feel tired. They have an "all or nothing" approach to life that may drive behaviors that make them feel good in the moment, but that comes from an instinctual impulse for gratification, for filling up an inner emptiness that can never be filled.

This lustful tendency to be excessive makes it easy for this type to lose the capacity to fine-tune their actions and to moderate their impact or their impatience. The influence of lust can also lead them to be excessively trusting and willing to assume that others are as truthful and sincere as they are.

If you identify with this type, here are some typical manifestations of lust you must observe and make more conscious to start down your path of awakening:

- Disputes connected to power; aiming to restore justice through your own strength of will.

- Excessively direct communication, sometimes experienced by the receiver as offensive or lacking empathy.

- Use of adverbs of intensity, capital letters, "bad" words, and language that expresses intensity and passion.

- Excessive certainty about things, including decisions; assuming your truth is the truth.

- Provoking people and rebelling against rules, authority, or established norms of behavior.

- Getting physically close to people; establishing intense eye contact.

- Automatically expanding your energy beyond your body when approaching someone; a tendency to be viewed as being "larger than life."

- An orientation toward the physical or concrete more than the subtle or abstract.

- Being constantly energized, full of life force, and resilient.

. . . .
"When going back makes sense, you are going ahead."
—Wendell Berry
. . . .

Using Type 8 Wings as Growth Stretches

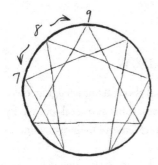

The two personality types adjacent to Type 8 on the Enneagram circle are Types 7 and 9. This type can learn to moderate their energy and intensity by leaning into Type 7's tendency to lead with charm and levity, and then learn to balance their over-assertion of their own point of view by integrating the adaptable and easygoing qualities of Type 9. This helps them move beyond their need for power and broaden their usual perspective.

- First, reach toward Type 7 by dialing down your intensity and focusing more on engaging with others in enjoyable ways. Find ways to make your interactions more interesting and learn how to take things more easily. Soften your approach by making conscious efforts to be playful or to use humor when you communicate. Consider adopting a more innovative mindset, rather than always leading with forcefulness or certainty. Balance your action orientation with an effort to be more rational and imaginative. Share more of your own experiences and dreams as a way of making yourself more approachable and open in relating to others.

• Then adopt Type 9's ability to listen to others and make sure they feel heard by you. Balance your usual confidence in your own perspective with a sincere effort to consider others' viewpoints. Truly take in what others say and let their opinions impact your plans. Be less of a leader and more of a follower. Become more empathetic by paying attention to what others want and tying your plans to what benefits them. Be more diplomatic and understanding when you communicate to avoid conflicts.

· ·

"Only in the darkness can you see the stars."
—Martin Luther King Jr.

· ·

Facing the Shadow

The second part of the Type 8 growth journey is all about acknowledging, owning, and integrating an awareness of their softer emotions and weak points. By learning to live and lead more from a more conscious sense of their own vulnerability, they can move forward on their journey.

It takes great strength to be vulnerable. When Type 8s realize that their focus on making things happen means that they sometimes don't listen to others or understand their impact, they gain self-awareness and come to see how they can be overbearing, aggressive, and dismissive, even while they may believe they are just being fierce, protective, and bold. When they exert too much strength and power, they can be blind to their impact and the subtle nuances of their social interactions. But by owning these shadow aspects, they can integrate more of a positive sense of their own sensitivity and begin to enjoy a life in which vulnerability can be a path to joy and happiness.

Meeting the Type 8 Shadow

If you identify as a Type 8, here are some actions you can take to bring to the surface, become more aware of, and start working to counteract the key unconscious patterns, blind spots, and pain points of the type:

- Take concrete steps toward self-disclosing with others. You probably actually trust very few people. It takes time for you to trust others and, if they betray you, you may find it impossible to forgive. This may be one way that you avoid feeling vulnerable. Challenge yourself to take the risk to open up more to those you trust and perhaps to others as well.

- Focus on the good things about people you meet. Your confrontational style may be more judgmental than you admit. Without realizing it, you may confront first and seek reasons later. Stop instinctively identifying objectionable traits to oppose in others and be more optimistic about what they have to offer you.

- Get in touch with the exhaustion you feel from being so strong and competent all the time. Stop denying the ways lust can deplete you, and take better care of yourself. Allow life to direct your actions rather than imposing your will to move things forward.

- Let go of your tendency to go against people you perceive as offending you (or others you care about). This may stem from vengeance, though you may rationalize your response as fighting for justice. Do more to create peace rather than war, even if you consciously believe your warrior efforts serve a good cause.

- Get feedback from others about what's really true when appraising important situations. When you believe your first impressions too easily, this puts you in danger of being wrong at least some of the time.

Question your arrogant (or naive) assumption that you have the only correct view of things.

- Stop overprotecting people in your life and doing too much for them. If you see others as weak or fragile, they may not develop their own strength. And when you project your own fragility onto them as a way of denying it, you avoid seeing and addressing your own weaknesses.

- Stop and laugh at yourself when you start measuring your own power against others'. Not everything needs to be viewed as a test of wills or a power struggle. Try to focus less on establishing a power base. You may create unnecessary conflicts or opposition when you proactively take a stance that pits you against others out of habit.

- Pause before going into action. Notice if you have a "ready, fire, aim" approach to life. Practice waiting for a short period of time before you say something to someone or make a big decision. Go for a walk before reacting, especially when you feel really angry.

- Learn to moderate your actions and reactions. You may come on too strong at times or intimidate people without intending to, and you may not be able to discern the impact of your powerful energy. Practice managing your emotions and containing your energy when facing situations in which you may want to temper your impact.

. . . .

"Everything that we see is a shadow cast by that which we do not see." —Martin Luther King Jr.

. . . .

The Type 8 Blind Spots

This type may not want to examine their blind spots because they may be fine with their personality's normal operating procedures—since they often keep them in control and in charge. As an 8, however, you show real strength (and wisdom) when you question whether you can be *too* sure of yourself in a way that ultimately doesn't serve your growth. Your ego's usual perspective makes you think that you always know best and you can (and should) always get your way— even if you may have to overpower someone or push to make it happen.

But here's the good news if you are an 8. If you can be humble and open enough to look more closely at the aspects of your survival strategy that you don't easily see, you can balance your powerful approach to life with an ability to be softer, more approachable, and more available for connection. If you can allow yourself to recognize what is holding you back from being more available to and more known by others, you can express more of the generosity, warmth, and care that abound in your big heart.

Here are some of the specific unconscious patterns that operate as blind spots that you must confront as a Type 8 to wake up from your zombie mode.

Denying Vulnerability

Do you tend not to feel some of the softer human emotions like sadness, fear, doubt, hurt, and insecurity? Do you unconsciously avoid most emotions that might make you feel vulnerable or weak? Do you believe that it's not okay to express any kind of weakness? And does this prohibition against feeling weak lead you to cut off your access to your softer emotions?

Here are some steps you can take to integrate this blind spot:

- Notice what emotions you rarely or almost never feel. Ask people you trust for feedback about what they observe in you when it comes to emotional expression.

- Allow yourself to challenge any belief you hold that it's not okay to be weak, and explore the consequences of that belief in your life.

- Recognize and talk about your softer emotions with people you trust. Allow yourself to develop more contact with feelings like sadness, hurt, and pain, with the knowledge that these are important human emotions that help us connect more deeply with others and with our own depths.

- Notice if you try to avoid registering vulnerable emotions and sometimes express too much strength and power as a way of compensating for unacknowledged vulnerabilities. Notice if you become more excessive the more you deny your vulnerability, thus remaining unaware of important experiences and aspects of yourself.

- Allow yourself to get in touch with any fears you may have. Develop more understanding of the positive uses of fear, including how it can help you identify dangers and threats. Notice if you put yourself in risky situations unnecessarily because you don't allow yourself to register fear.

- Observe whether you tend to deny feelings you see as "weak," without considering how that impacts you. Recognize how sensitive you actually are. Do "inner child" work to get in touch with the vulnerable part of yourself that you tend to deny unconsciously out of a need to express strength in the world.

- Remind yourself continually that only a person who is truly strong has the capacity to feel vulnerable.

Not Understanding Your Impact on Others

Do you make people feel disturbed, upset, or hurt when you think you are simply being honest or passionate? Are you sometimes surprised to learn that people are intimidated by you when that was not your intention? Do you sometimes not know your own strength, or not know how much force to use? Are you sometimes unaware of the effect you have on people?

Here are some things you can do to integrate this blind spot:

- Pay close attention to input when you talk to others. Be alert for any signs of how people feel based on their facial expressions or other forms of nonverbal communication.

- Apologize when someone tells you they felt hurt by you. While it can be hard to say you're sorry, the ability to show remorse expands your possibilities for connection with others and allows you to tap into the vulnerability you may experience when hurting someone or feeling regret.

- Ask someone you trust to give you honest and direct feedback about your impact on others. We all need to hear how people experience us to know how to fine-tune our communication and achieve the impact we want to have.

- Whenever you become aware of trouble in a relationship, find out as soon as possible if you did anything hurtful or upsetting. If you hear that you did, don't push back, just listen and try to understand the truth of what happened.

- Consciously lower your energy level when approaching others. Pay closer attention to how you feel. Practice containing your energy by imagining that you gather it into yourself and hold it in.

- Train yourself to smile more and appear more relaxed. Notice how this shifts your interactions.

Assuming Your Truth Equals *The* Truth

Do you tend to believe that your own subjective view of things is the objective truth? Do you tend to evaluate—or act to resolve—unfair situations based on the assumption that your judgments about what is right and wrong are accurate? Do you tend to deny any aspects of what's happening that don't fit with the way you want to see things? Are you unaware that you have biases that may distort your views?

Here are some things you can do to integrate this blind spot:

- Ask yourself why you believe that you know what's right and wrong in whatever situation you are in—why you often think you hold the correct opinion and others don't.

- Examine your own conclusions more carefully and more often to see if you have considered all the information available. Look back at your life to find situations in which you thought you were right, but you weren't.

- Stop yourself before you speak or take action. Be patient and humble enough to listen carefully to the opinions of others you trust about the best course of action.

- Allow yourself to be open to the validity and wisdom of other points of view.

- When you discuss an issue about which you have a clear opinion, ask more questions, make fewer affirmations, and consider other possibilities.

- Ask yourself these questions the next time you come to a firm conclusion about an important situation: Have you really tried to put yourself in the other person's shoes? Are there any factors you may not have considered? Are you jumping too quickly to a judgment without knowing all the facts?

. . . .

"Vulnerability is not winning or losing; it's having the courage to show up and be seen when we have no control over the outcome." —Brené Brown

. . . .

Type 8 Pain

This personality type usually feels as if they have endless energy and a boundless capacity to do all they want to do. They put all their focus on a highly positive vision of all they can be and do, without acknowledging their normal human limitations. But this comes at a price. Without knowing it, their denial of weakness or limits leads them to overvalue their ability to do whatever they want and undervalue their basic human emotions. This means they may hurt themselves and be hurt by others while avoiding any consciousness of their pain. While this habitual denial of pain or suffering allows them to be effective in life in some ways, it prevents them from feeling all they need to feel to grow.

One of the main tasks for Type 8s is to get in touch with their vulnerable emotions and make contact with the pain they hold in their bodies and their hearts. For the sake of their self-development, they must become more vulnerable, respect the limits of their bodies, and attend to the softer needs of their hearts. When they decide to face their pain, they take important steps toward becoming more mature, more healthy, and more whole. When they learn to express their weaknesses, they become truly strong. When they balance their power with an awareness of their sensitivity, they allow themselves to experience a sense of inner peace and relaxation they never knew existed.

If you identify with this type, you hide a soft, vulnerable, deep, warm, defenseless, caring, beautiful, and very human person underneath your "armor"—the real you. But you will need help from people you trust to shed that armor. This will be difficult and you will need to be reassured that you are "okay." Remember that, by intentionally accessing vulnerable emotions, you demonstrate the true level of your bravery. Here are some of the painful feelings you must let yourself feel to wake up out of your zombie mode:

- Fear that people will take advantage of you. Fully feeling this fear has the power to bring you more in touch with your heart so you can access your vulnerability.

- Pain and hurt that you resist. When you lower your defenses, you can welcome back your sensitivity and feel the stored-up pain that has always been there, but that you have denied. When you acknowledge pain connected to feeling unprotected, unsupported, disregarded, hurt, or wounded, you can move past your need to be strong. Stay in touch with the truth of this and talk about it with a therapist or a close friend. Take in the care and love you deserve. Have compassion for yourself for all you did to protect your sensitivity when you didn't even know it existed. Protect yourself from people who won't understand or respect the shift they see in you when you open up to your sensitivity.

- Exhaustion from overextending your physical and emotional capacities when you try to do more than is humanly possible. It takes a toll on your body when you act as if you are indestructible and express strength without awareness of your limits.

- Confusion about your identity when you no longer feel as strong as you did before, even though you don't want to put your old armor back on.

- Insecurity because of doubts about what to do. This can be a healthy thing. While it may sound bad, this helps you to grow in the right direction. Your old survival strategies made you believe you could always do more for everyone. Now, you need to tell others that you are not made of iron.

. . . .

"Holding on to anger is like drinking poison and expecting the other person to die." —Buddha

. . . .

The Type 8 Subtypes

Identifying your Type 8 subtype can help you more precisely target your efforts to confront your blind spots, unconscious tendencies, and hidden pain. The specific patterns and tendencies of the subtypes vary depending on which of the three survival instincts dominates your experience.

Self-Preservation 8 Subtype

This subtype is the most practical and pragmatic, and feels a strong need to get what's theirs and what they need for survival. They focus the most on material security. They excel at finding ways to get what they want to support their need to feel satisfied or secure. They may have a difficult time being patient and want immediate satisfaction of their needs and desires. They appear more reserved, guarded, or defended, and may seem more contained. They don't talk much.

Social 8 Subtype

This subtype exhibits some contradictory traits. They can rebel against social norms, but also offer protection, support, and loyalty to others. They appear more helpful and fight against injustice toward others. They take action to protect people who are being persecuted or exploited. They like the power that a group offers. They may look more mellow and friendly, and less quick to anger than the other Type 8 subtypes.

Sexual (One-to-One) 8 Subtype

This subtype is the most provocative and rebellious. They speak out against rules and tend to be more magnetic and charismatic. They are more emotional than the other Type 8 subtypes and tend to be very possessive of the people in their lives. They display more passion and action, and less thought. They energetically take over the whole scene and like being in control and being the center of attention.

The Type 8 Subtype Shadows

You can more effectively confront your own Shadow if you know the specific shadow characteristics of your subtype. Below are some of the shadow aspects of each subtype. As subtype behavior can be highly automatic and unconscious, these traits can be the hardest to see and own.

Self-Preservation 8 Shadow

If this is your subtype, you tend to be overly pragmatic and can sometimes become selfish. You likely know how to do business, and you may barter and bargain to get an advantage over others to get a good deal for yourself. You prioritize your own survival. You may give up exploring more of life and opening up more to others in order to maintain a sense of security. You may focus more on access to money and other resources than on relationships. You may unconsciously disqualify any feeling, person, idea, or institution that opposes your desires. As the most armored of the three subtypes, you have the hardest time allowing yourself to be vulnerable.

Social 8 Shadow

If this is your subtype, you often embody the archetype of the matriarch or the patriarch who takes care of everybody, although you may not see the cost of this. By disregarding your own well-being, you tend to sacrifice yourself. You may feel challenged when it comes to caring for yourself or allowing others to take care of you. You protect others, but don't get protected—and aren't always aware of this. You can't stop yourself from intervening when you see others being mistreated by someone who has more power. And while this savior role can seem noble and brave, it may not be good for you or your growth.

Sexual (One-to-One) 8 Shadow

If this is your subtype, you have the greatest need for power of all the twenty-seven Enneagram types. You seek to have power over everything and everyone. You have a need to possess people and their attention, which fuels your need to be at the center of everything that happens. You want to control people and you want them to submit to your control. As the most emotional of the Type 8 subtypes, you may not be aware that you act from impulse and passion, but often don't slow down enough to think about what you do.

> "We mature with the damage, not with the years."
> —Mateus William

The Type 8 Paradox

The Type 8 paradox is grounded in the polarity between the passion of lust and the virtue of innocence. This type must recognize the fear and sadness they hold within to transform. They must discover that their deeper emotions have been denied and hidden by lust. By acknowledging and owning this, they take an important step toward innocence and gain the ability to stay in touch with their vulnerability and open their hearts. Innocence opposes lust by allowing Type 8s to respond in a fresh way to each moment, free of expectations or judgments. It reflects the softness, calmness, and gentleness of the heart that does not need intensity to feel satisfied.

If you identify with this type, here are some things you can do at this stage of your growth journey to become more conscious of lust and start accessing the higher-level emotion of innocence:

- Notice if you speed up or withdraw to be alone when you start feeling vulnerable. Observe what feelings motivate these behaviors; admit that these feelings are normal and welcome them.

- Allow yourself to feel gradually more vulnerable. Let yourself feel "smaller" than your normal size.

- Make conscious efforts to communicate your vulnerability to others—first to those few people you really trust. Open up to how they respond to you.

- Ask people you trust for help or care. Make specific requests for what you need.

- Notice how your heart softens and your body relaxes when you do something hard like asking for help. Consider how this softening makes it impossible for you to react against anyone, and how you begin to see the goodness in other people more than before.

- Check to see what emotions live beneath your anger—and give them more space.

· ·

"We are never so vulnerable as when we love."
—Sigmund Freud

· ·

Using Type 8 Arrow Lines for Growth

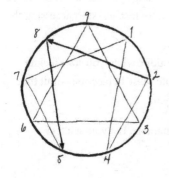

The two personality types connected to Type 8 by the internal arrow lines within the Enneagram diagram are Types 2 and 5. By developing Type 2's capacity to be softer and more emotional, you become kinder and more approachable; by integrating Type 5's ability to slow down and moderate your actions, you become less forceful and more contained. This helps you to create big growth shifts from your usual focus on being strong and fighting injustice, and directs your focus inward so you can balance your energy.

- First, intentionally embody Type 2's ability to pay more attention to other people's feelings and allow yourself to become softer, gentler, kinder, and more approachable. Learn to be less blunt and more careful and diplomatic in what you say. Deepen your connections with others by making sure you listen more and share more of what you are feeling. Pay attention to what others need and make an effort to empathize with their feelings. Tie your plans to what benefits others.

- Then integrate Type 5's ability to think before taking action. Notice any urges you may have to control others and allow for more independence. Learn how to be less intense and more contained. Go inward more to balance out your energy. Do research and consult expert sources to confirm or counter your view before you make decisions.

> "It's tougher to be vulnerable than to actually be tough."
> —Rihanna

EMBRACING THE HIGH SIDE

On the third part of their journey, 8s begin to see more clearly who they are *not*. By remembering what it feels like to be more in contact with their sensitivity, they start to see the wisdom in embracing their softer side. They dare to show up in a lighter way, without as much protection. They put down their weapons instead of remaining guarded and aggressive. When they have done this, they learn to walk more slowly through life. They learn to take better care of themselves. They learn to welcome and appreciate more of their own emotions—and to empathize more with others' emotions without having to do anything about them. They understand that the best way to process emotions is just to be present with them.

Ironically, this makes Type 8s seem even stronger and more powerful than before. As they discover that it takes great courage and strength to express vulnerability, they move forward on their path. And this shift is often noticed by others. Being in touch with their own sensitivity naturally balances out their tendency to exert brute force in the world and to take charge or control things.

If you identify with this type, here are some things you can do on this part of your journey that you couldn't have done before—and what you can continue to work on:

- Make contact with vulnerable feelings in a conscious way more often.

- Appreciate details and subtleties that you previously overlooked.

- Listen to others more fully.

- Develop more patience—with yourself and others.

- Respect your own limitations. Take better care of yourself physically and psychologically.

- Approach people with more sensitivity than before; be more careful with your words and in how you treat people.

- Reduce your tendency to act on impulse—to do things that you may regret later.

- Be less excessive in the things you do; develop your ability to moderate your actions and your energy.

- Empathize more with others; understand more how others feel by accessing a wider range of emotions inside yourself. Connect more deeply with people.

"Vulnerability is not weakness. And that myth is profoundly dangerous. Vulnerability is the birthplace of innovation, creativity, and change." —Brené Brown

The Type 8 Virtue

Innocence is the virtue that provides an antidote to the Type 8 passion of lust. In a state of innocence, this type becomes less guarded and aggressive and gains a newfound heart-based capacity to stay undefended. This allows them to stop being so intense and excessive in life and relationships. They respond to people and situations rather than reacting to them. They have a more positive outlook and know that conditions (and people) will not be as harsh as they expect. They trust that others—and they themselves—are inherently good, not bad. They no longer need to be in charge of everything or override life's natural rhythms. They realize that, if they stay nonreactive and disclose themselves to others more, they will not be attacked. They, in a sense, learn to disarm others by putting down their own weapons first. And they no longer allow other people's aggression to determine their state of being.

If you identify with this type, here are some things you must focus on to move forward on your journey toward living more from a state of innocence.

- Responding in a new way to each thing that happens.

- Bringing no expectations based in the past to new experiences—like a baby who forgets about pain right after it goes away.

- Slowing your pace to take in and appreciate the details and nuances of what happens around you.

- Bringing more sensitivity to your experience of everything and everyone.

- Tuning in to sensitivity and to the emotional level of experience.

- Becoming acutely aware of every little impact you have on others and the world around you, and having a greater capacity to listen and to create peace.

- Calibrating your energy; making adjustments to your power so you apply just the right amount of force in each thing you do.

- Letting go of your defensive need to judge others and releasing your tendency to judge yourself or be harsh with yourself in any way.

- Feeling free from the anger that used to control you and finally becoming harmless.

. . . .

"When we were children, we used to think that when we were grown up we would no longer be vulnerable. But to grow up is to accept vulnerability." —Madeleine L'Engle

. . . .

Waking Up from the Zombie State

For Type 8s, the key to embracing the true self lies in relaxing their bodies using their breath—and in feeling like a normal-sized person as opposed to feeling "larger than life." When this type connects more regularly to their inner experience—and their sensitivity—they naturally allow their energy to become more contained and less expansive. They can still have a powerful impact on others and the world around them, but now their power comes from an amazing blend of true strength and genuine softness that reveals their authentic selves.

As this type advances on the path of self-development, they become beautifully sensitive. When they balance their natural intensity with a capacity to contact vulnerability, they develop a high level of personal power and magnetism that allows them to connect with and inspire others in the deepest way possible. The state of innocence encourages others to be close to them and to share their truths, which is what they had hoped for all along.

By managing to be both vulnerable and innocent, Type 8s are initiated into a whole new experience of life. They realize that they don't always need to be powerful, because others will support them. This new reality brings them the joy of contacting and loving their inner child, and seeing how life rewards them for developing the greatest strength of all—the ability to be strong enough to show weakness. By revealing their weakness, they become powerful beyond measure, fully capable of deploying their power with sensitivity and empathy for others. They realize how good it feels to surrender to a power larger than their own, and to let go of their need to correct all the unfairness and injustice in the world. As they begin to experience their true selves, 8s become simpler, lighter, warmer, and more available to others in a deeper way. They no longer feel the zombie's need to engage with life from excess: life can be lived as it comes.

If you identify with this type, your awakening involves no longer needing to protect yourself against injustices or fortify yourself to safeguard your sensitivity, because nothing can really harm you at this more essential level. When you know more of your real self, you experience yourself as even more delicate and softer than you imagined. You don't need to wear armor anymore. Your connection to your own depths and to others shows that you no longer need to react or attack; you can relax and trust more. When this happens, you connect to a much greater clarity about how good and beautiful people are deep inside—including, most of all, yourself. You can finally allow the full force of your heart—and your inherent emotional sensitivity—to shine forth. You can express all the love that was always there behind the armor. For Type 8s, this feels like a rebirth into a new life of receptivity, contemplation, simplicity, love, and gratitude.

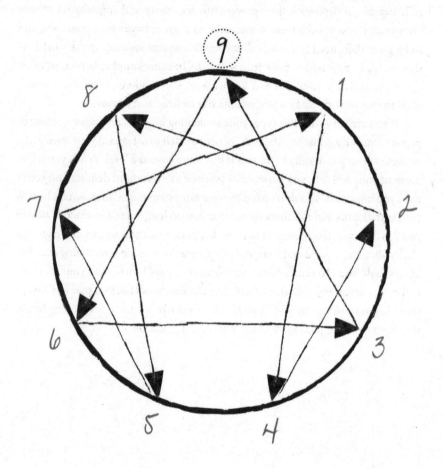

The Path from Sloth to Right Action

Be there for others, but never leave yourself behind.

<small>DODINSKY</small>

O nce upon a time, there was a person named Nine. Early in life, he felt connected to everyone and everything, as if there were no such thing as separation. In this state of unity, Nine felt a deep sense of peace, joy, and love that was wonderful and deeply comforting.

But then something happened. Nine woke up one day feeling alone and disconnected. He felt frustrated at having been left by himself and wanted to register a protest against whoever had pushed him out on his own. But this made him even more uncomfortable. There were others nearby, but they seemed somehow distant. This new sense of being separate felt lonely and scary. If he was no longer connected to the world around him, how could he feel any sense of belonging?

When Nine tried to complain about this new and disturbing situation in order to re-establish his connection with others, no one would listen. Those around him spoke louder and had more important things to say. They knew what they wanted and argued to get it. They didn't seem bothered by the fact that they were separate—and that their arguing made them more so. They didn't seem to care what Nine was saying. He tried speaking louder and protesting more, but no one paid attention. After a while, he simply gave up. If they weren't going to listen, he might as well go back to sleep. At least there was comfort in sleep.

Nine kept sleeping and trying to find comfort. But this sensation of not being connected stayed with him, and he grew concerned that he would never be included again. He wondered what his feelings of separation said about him.

Others didn't seem as bothered by it as he did. Then he found that, when he stopped trying to get people's attention—when he distracted himself somehow—he felt more comfortable.

Nine tried different ways to approximate the sense of connection he had lost, hoping to recover some of his feelings of belonging. He made friends and did whatever they wanted him to do. He tried to blend in. He tried to forget the distance he felt by focusing on what others wanted and forgetting about his own desires. He stopped confronting people with whom he disagreed, because he found it was easier just to go along with whatever they said. And after a while, he found he didn't really care that much anyway. It didn't really seem that important. *He* didn't really seem that important.

Over time, Nine's survival strategy of staying quiet and comfortable to avoid the pain of his separate existence caused him to forget all about his own feelings, his own opinions, and his own voice. He would rather get along with people. Staying comfortable was just so much more—well, comfortable. And being in harmony with others brought him a vague memory of the connection he had lost. After a while, it even seemed as if, even though he "woke up" each day, he was really sleep-walking through life.

Every once in a while, Nine tried sharing an opinion or a desire with the people around him so they could get to know him better and connect with him. But no one seemed to listen, which just made him feel separate again. Eventually, he realized that he no longer knew exactly what his opinions were or what he wanted. And that made him feel uncomfortable as well. Sometimes he felt bothered by the fact that everyone expected him to go along with whatever they wanted. And he worried that he no longer knew what *he* wanted. He even felt a little anger at not being heard or considered important. He tried expressing this anger once, but that just made people move even farther away. Apparently no one liked to connect with angry people. And that made him feel even more disconnected and alone. So Nine's survival strategy of staying quiet and unaware of his own inner experience took over, and he just went back to sleep.

Nine had become a zombie—a very peaceful, easygoing, comfort-loving zombie, but a zombie just the same.

THE TYPE 9 CHECKLIST

If most or all of the following personality traits apply to you, you may be a Type 9:

- ☑ You like it when everyone around you gets along harmoniously and there is no tension.

- ☑ You get along with most people pretty well and find it easy to blend in with the agendas of others.

- ☑ You don't like to disturb the peace and excel at mediating or avoiding conflicts.

- ☑ You only rarely express anger in an open, direct way.

- ☑ You can see many sides of an issue and easily understand different perspectives.

- ☑ You naturally support the people around you, not to get recognition for yourself, but just to be helpful and promote a peaceful environment.

- ☑ People tell you they find you easygoing, friendly, and easy to be around.

- ☑ You often find it hard to know what you want. You may sense there is a "fog" around you that doesn't let you see your own desires. However, it's a little easier to know what you don't want.

- ☑ Although you don't always speak up or offer your opinion, you don't like it when people overlook or exclude you. You dislike it when people are authoritarian and tell you what to do.

If, after using this checklist, you find that you are a Type 9, your growth journey will follow three steps.

First, you will embark on the quest to know yourself by identifying personality patterns associated with staying comfortable and doing whatever you need to do to get along with the people around you.

Then you must face your Shadow to become more aware of ego patterns that stem from your feelings of disconnection and your sense of feeling unimportant. This helps you see how you forget yourself when you over-adapt to others as a way to maintain harmony and avoid separation.

The final stage of your journey involves getting more fully in touch with your anger, your desires, and your priorities, and learning how important you actually are.

. . . .
"People say nothing is impossible, but I do nothing
every day." —Winnie the Pooh
. . . .

EMBARKING ON THE QUEST

The first stage of awakening for this type involves intentionally noticing how they make themselves unimportant by putting themselves last. By becoming more conscious of how they focus their attention and energy on their environment and on anything external (people, things, and processes), they start to develop the capacity to self-reflect. This is especially important for Type 9s, as they tend to "fall asleep to themselves" and forget to pay attention to their own experience. They sometimes sleep-walk through life as a way to deaden themselves to their own feelings and sense of separation.

Key Type 9 Patterns

If you identify as a Type 9, your journey starts by recognizing how much energy you devote to maintaining a sense of harmony and connection with the world around you, and how little attention you focus on your own being and agenda. You must become more conscious of all the ways you try to avoid any kind of discomfort and become more aware of what exactly feels comfortable and uncomfortable to you.

To launch your journey of awakening, focus on and make more conscious these five habitual Type 9 patterns.

Neglecting What Is Important to You

You tend to support others and pay attention to all sorts of external demands, but neglect your own needs and priorities. It will be important for you to notice if you prioritize other people's agendas over your own. It may be hard for you to act on your own personal priorities, rather than work on tasks connected to others, routines and processes, and other less important activities in life. You may habitually minimize your own importance. Even when you don't like the way life seems to make you unimportant, it may be hard for you to assert yourself. Your tendency to avoid conflict might also lead you to minimize your own preferences and perspectives. It will help you to see if it is difficult for you to know what you want, and if this makes you feel disappointed and frustrated.

Difficulty Mobilizing Your Energy on Your Own Behalf

You may find that you can easily mobilize your energy when you are helping others, but you have a hard time sustaining your focus and energy when acting on your own behalf. You may find it difficult to take action in support of (or even know) what *you* need and want. You benefit from noticing if it is hard for you to clarify your own agenda and sustain your efforts to pursue it. You may get distracted when you try to make a conscious effort to do what you need to do for yourself. You probably prioritize less essential tasks, rather then paying attention to and acting on what is really meaningful to you.

Difficulty Establishing Boundaries

You may notice that you have difficulty saying "no" to people when they want you to do something for them. This may be another way in which you put others before yourself or over-adapt to what others want. It will be good for you to notice if it is hard for you to go against people or speak up when you don't agree. You may have trouble setting limits when people take too much of your attention and energy. And all of these tendencies may highlight the fact that you have a difficult time seeing your need for boundaries and establishing them in your relationships with others.

Avoiding Conflict and Disharmony

You may notice you have a natural ability to be energetically attuned to the level of harmony or disharmony in your world. You tend to try to create harmony with the people around you and you work against conflict, disharmony, or tension of any kind. In fact, you may feel bothered by people who inject tension into the environment by creating problems or disturbing the peace. You typically work to avoid conflicts you might have with others or mediate conflicts among the people in your immediate environment. Your gift for helping people understand each other is motivated by a desire to help everyone get along. It will be important to notice if you you feel driven to fulfill the wishes of others as a way to keep things peaceful and stay connected to the important people in your life. And it will be important for you to notice if your need to avoid conflict ends up keeping you asleep to yourself.

Avoiding Discomfort

You may notice you have a tendency always to try to stay comfortable and avoid what feels uncomfortable. You may establish routines to stay comfortable, and try to avoid threats to your comfort, including disruptions, disagreements with others, or change of any kind. You tend to avoid uncomfortable feelings and sensations— and also avoid conflict and an awareness of your own anger as part of the effort to prevent discomfort. When you observe yourself in an intentional, ongoing way, you will likely discover that you prioritize staying in your comfort zone.

> "In order to act consciously with the intention of awakening, it is necessary to know the nature of the forces which keep man in a state of sleep." —G. I. Gurdjieff

The Type 9 Passion

Sloth is the passion that drives Type 9. As the core emotional motivation of this type, sloth is a kind of laziness—not in the usual sense of not wanting to do things, but rather a reluctance to take important actions for themselves that are needed in the moment. This is usually an action that should be taken to support their own needs, but it can also be any first step that can change the reality around them. Through sloth, 9s consistently and unconsciously neglect themselves and their potential role in making a difference in the world.

This type has a tendency to pay attention mainly to things outside of themselves and to forget about their own inner experience, to the point that they have a hard time knowing what they think, feel, and want. When you ask them what they want, they often don't know. They may have difficulty even knowing basic things about themselves, like what they want to eat for dinner. They can be very active in supporting others, but get caught in inertia and lose energy when it comes to acting in support of themselves. Their tendency to operate on autopilot and "forget" about their own priorities leads them to disconnect from their own needs, desires, feelings, opinions, and preferences, as well as their power to make change in the world. Under the influence of sloth, they deaden themselves—put themselves to sleep—to avoid having to "show up" and ask for attention in a world they believe sees them as unimportant. This drive to put the focus on others causes an unwillingness to have any kind of agenda at all. It expresses a kind of "giving up" on the effort to tune in to themselves.

Type 9s often take "the path of least resistance" when it comes to their own agendas—a reflection of sloth's tendency to put out minimal effort. They "go with the flow" rather than assert their own priorities, often to the point of losing awareness of what their own priorities might be. They focus on making things comfortable and easy for others as well as themselves, which includes avoiding conflict as well as deeper engagements with people.

If you identify with this type, you must observe and make conscious these typical manifestations of sloth to move forward on your path to awakening:

- An inability or unwillingness to attend to your inner world—a kind of laziness about being aware of what's going on inside. A lack of interest in tapping into your moment-to-moment experience.

- Self-neglect and "self-forgetting" in all forms, including emotional, psychological, and physical.

- Doing more of the same and resisting any change when it comes to courses of action that are already in motion.

- Feeling unimportant and not putting yourself in the picture; not considering what you want and need as a consequence.

- Procrastination when it comes to big priorities, including those most important to you personally.

- Not knowing what you want; not having or expressing opinions or desires. Putting out a lot of energy to support others, but not having much for yourself.

- Resignation about getting what you need and want. Proactively giving up on receiving anything, while going along with others and helping them get what they want.

- A lack of emotional experience in your connection with yourself and others that is usually perceived only by people who are truly close to you.

- Discomfort with being the center of attention or drawing attention to yourself by asking for anything or expressing preferences.

. . . .
"You cannot find peace by avoiding life." —Virginia Woolf
. . . .

Using Type 9 Wings as Growth Stretches

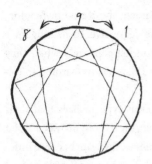

The two personality types adjacent to Type 9 on the Enneagram circle are Types 8 and 1. To move beyond their tendency to "go to sleep" to themselves, this type can begin to channel their frustration in more assertive ways by expressing Type 8 traits, and then get more in touch with their own priorities by integrating the strengths of Type 1.

- First, incorporate positive Type 8 traits by turning up the volume on any irritation or stubbornness you may feel and channeling it into more assertive forms of communication. See the big picture, sense what you want, and ask for it in a clear, direct manner. Develop more confidence and skill in expressing your opinions or "going against" others. Increase your tolerance for constructive conflict. Learn to voice concerns and initiate discussions about problems in your relationships. Notice how being decisive, confronting issues head-on, and acknowledging disagreements can lead to stronger connections rather than separation. Become aware of all the many positive uses of anger.

- Then integrate Type 1's ability to envision a high-quality outcome for an agenda you create to address your priorities. Become more in touch with your preferences and needs by taking some time to imagine the best possible result and working backward from there. Stay focused on personal goals and tasks by developing a structure based on a logical series of actions. Increase your willingness to execute on your own ideal agenda by seeing more clearly how your efforts connect to a larger vision of making things better for everyone. Get in touch with anger at what's not right and channel it to create reforms that make the world a better place.

. . . .

"Procrastination is opportunity's assassin." —Victor Kiam

. . . .

FACING THE SHADOW

The second part of the Type 9 growth journey is largely about acknowledging, accepting, and integrating the tendency to be passive-aggressive. By making their anger more conscious, 9s learn that true connection happens only when they take the risk to know and express themselves, even if that means learning to tolerate the fear of separation.

In this more advanced stage of their journey, this type realizes that their focus on adapting to and supporting others (which they thought was a good thing) can be a bad thing. When they lack self-awareness, they can become indecisive, overly passive, and passive-aggressive, even while they consciously believe they are being nice, friendly, and inoffensive. When they fail to see their blind spots, they can become stubborn and disengaged. When they don't like what's happening, they tend to avoid expressing their dissatisfaction directly. But this leads them to engage in passive-aggressive behavior when their unacknowledged anger leaks out in passive forms. For instance, they may disappear when they are most needed and not do what they said they were going to do.

Meeting the Type 9 Shadow

If you identify as a Type 9, here are some actions you can take to bring to the surface, become more aware of, and start to counteract the key unconscious patterns, blind spots, and pain points of this type:

- Bring your attention to what feels uncomfortable. Do things that bring discomfort, knowing that this is your path of growth. Notice how you tend to resist leaving your comfort zone. Start to step outside it in small ways, then in larger ways.

- Allow yourself to get more in touch with anger. Be more aware of whatever makes you upset and how you put your anger to sleep. Start noticing repressed or passive forms of anger like irritation, frustration, and stubbornness. Welcome anger as a way to reconnect to what is important to you. Take the risk to communicate anger more directly.

- Notice all the ways you are passive, passively resistant, and passive-aggressive (including being stubborn). Ask for feedback from people you trust about any ways they experience these tendencies in you.

- Recall an incident in which you felt dissatisfied, upset, or unhappy. Take notes about how you felt; consider what you said and what you didn't say but might have said.

- Use your capacity to sense your body to increase your energy level. Move more—walk, do yoga, or engage in any form of exercise. Let your increased body awareness help you become more active and invigorated.

- Think about and sense all the energy that you have given away and reclaim it by inhaling, focusing inside yourself, and feeling your strength.

- Take action to establish boundaries with others. Say "no" more. Stop saying "yes" when you mean "no." Be less nice, friendly, and smiley.

. . . .
"If we're growing, we're always going to be out of our comfort zone." —John Maxwell
. . . .

The Type 9 Blind Spots

This type may not want to examine their blind spots because they dislike feeling discomfort. And facing what we habitually avoid being aware of tends to be uncomfortable. (This is why we avoid them in the first place.) The specific ways Type 9s function to create peace, avoid conflict, and maintain friendly relations with people lead them to deaden themselves to important aspects of their experience—like their anger and their desires. The need for comfort dominates their experience and keeps them from being motivated to gain access to deeper forms of connection—both with their own depths and with others. But here's the good news. If they can look at their blind spots and deal with any pain or discomfort that arises, they can eventually become very powerful and feel very good about their gifts and strengths.

This type has a great deal of energy, but they tend to give it away to others. They may even feel depressed because of how their survival strategies lead them to fall asleep to their inherent sense of aliveness. They cut themselves off from a deeper, more intense experience of life when they disconnect from any emotions that might create tensions with others. But if they can tolerate the fear of their own power and energy—and the fear that they might hurt someone if they express how angry they actually are—they can redirect their energy more consciously for their own benefit in a way that will make a real difference in the world.

If you identify with Type 9, here are some of the blind spots you must become more aware of and start to integrate in order to move forward on your growth journey.

Avoiding Anger

Do you rarely get angry? Have you have actually "gone to sleep" to your anger? Do you avoid becoming aware of your anger because expressing it might lead to conflict? Have you considered the costs of this? Here are some actions you can take to integrate this blind spot:

- Notice when you feel small signs of anger or tamped-down forms of anger, like frustration, irritation, or stubbornness. Turn up the volume on all forms of anger, no matter how subtle.

- Realize that, when you don't consciously feel and express your anger, it doesn't go away; it leaks out as passive aggression. Learn to recognize when you are leaking.

- Become more aware of how and when you express aggression passively. Make lists of things you can do to be more active and direct in these situations, even if you are not ready to take these actions.

- Explore all the reasons why you don't want to feel or express anger—both generally and because of experiences in your past. Talk about this with a friend or therapist.

- Ask the people in your life to help you learn to express anger. Tell them about any fears you may have connected with being angry. Take the risk to start expressing your anger in small ways, being careful at the beginning. Learn how to express your frustration or disagreement as soon as it happens, so that it doesn't build up.

- Reframe anger as a good thing. When it's channeled consciously, it can help you establish boundaries, assert your needs, know what's most important, and access power.

Not Knowing What You Want

Do you often have no idea what you want? Do you go along with the agendas of others because you don't know or can't express your own desires or opinions? Do you tend not to have an agenda? Do you have trouble communicating what you want? Here are some actions you can take to integrate this blind spot:

- Ask yourself what you want more often. Keep asking, even if you don't yet have an answer. And remember to ask this of your heart, not just your head. The heart knows more than the head about wishes and desires.

- Remind yourself that it's okay not to know what you want. With time and consistent effort, you can learn to access your preferences.

- Don't judge yourself for not yet knowing what you want.

- Ask the people in your life to inquire about what you want, to express interest in knowing what you want, and to give you time to figure out what you want.

- Express opinions more often, even if you don't feel that strongly about what you say. Work against your tendency to see every perspective as equally valid. Push yourself to choose a side.

- Next time you say that you don't really care what happens, question whether this is how you rationalize not knowing what you want, not feeling the pain of not knowing what you want, and not doing the work of figuring out what you want. This is a potential manifestation of your passion of sloth.

Avoiding Conflict

Do you find many ways to avoid conflict? Do you make excuses for avoiding conflict? Does your avoidance of conflict limit you and the people around you? Here are some things you can do to integrate this blind spot:

- Explore your beliefs about conflict. Explore all your fears related to conflict. What do you fear will happen if you engage in conflict?

- Notice if you fear conflict because you believe it will inevitably lead to (potentially permanent) separation. Challenge this belief. Stay open to evidence that conflict can bring you closer to people. Learn to tell the difference between lack of conflict and true harmony. Deep and lasting peace is usually achieved through positive confrontation.

- Learn about and explore all the positive uses of conflict—supporting healthy boundaries, deepening relationships, and letting people know where you stand.

- Practice "leaning into" conflict to express disagreement and make yourself more known, more important, and more included as who you really are.

- Engage in conflict in small ways by saying "no" and establishing healthy boundaries.

- Allow yourself to "go against" people or what's happening as a way of expressing your power. Allow yourself to feel bothered, upset, or angry about situations you don't like.

. . . .

"It is love alone that leads to right action." —Krishnamurti

. . . .

Type 9 Pain

This type tends to be friendly and positive, and to focus on getting along with others. Their priority of avoiding conflict of all kinds means they are motivated to stay comfortable by maintaining a sense of peace and avoiding feeling specific emotions. To connect harmoniously with others, they habitually "go to sleep" to anger and related emotions that might cause tension. Because of this, they tend to appear "emotionally steady." They usually seem warm and good-natured and usually aren't very emotional. But in order to awaken, they must make deeper contact with their emotions. As body-based, "self-forgetting" types, they may need to make intentional efforts to connect with their pain. By getting in touch with suffering, 9s start to acknowledge their own emotions and learn not to neglect their depths. After all, it's harder to stay asleep when your body is energized by anger or saturated with sadness.

If you identify with this type, it may be difficult for you to experience emotions that disturb your comfort or threaten interpersonal harmony. But to move forward on your growth journey, you must learn to contact and tolerate these specific painful feelings to gain a fuller realization of your true self. Here are some of the feelings it will be important for you to confront:

- Fear of anger, fear of hurting others, and fear of separation. When you start to become more self-aware, you will likely realize that you fear your anger. You may fear that, if you allow yourself to get angry, you will hurt someone. You may also fear that expressing your anger will create irreparable separation—that it will damage or destroy relationships. This may also reflect a fear of your own power and energy.

- Anger that you repress or ignore. You must get more in touch with feeling your anger. This can be difficult, as you "go to sleep" to your anger as part of your main survival strategy. But feeling and expressing anger are central to your feeling energized and waking up to who you really are. Your false self will resist this, but it is absolutely necessary that you learn to feel and express anger and become aware of all the ways that anger leaks out in passive forms when you remain unconscious of it. When you really get in touch with all the anger in your Shadow, you go from thinking that you almost never get angry, to realizing that you are angry all the time. And this is a good thing.

- Grief and sadness over not being included, not belonging, or feeling overlooked or not heard. This is usually more intense if you are a social 9 subtype (see below). You may also feel grief at having hurt people without realizing it—for instance, when your avoidance of conflict, passive-aggression, and pursuit of harmony actually cause disharmony and injure people in ways you don't see. You need to experience grief and sadness to open your heart fully and awaken to more of your emotional depths.

- Pain at not being connected to your own sense of being—at not being able to know what you want and more deeply connect with yourself. You may also benefit from getting more in touch with the pain of disconnection that you tend to avoid. Sometimes disconnection can be a good thing—for instance, when you are connected to things and people that aren't good for you.

. . . .

"The Shadow is the greatest teacher for how to
come to the light." —Ram Dass

. . . .

The Type 9 Subtypes

Identifying your Type 9 subtype can help you target your efforts to confront your blind spots, unconscious tendencies, and hidden pain. The specific patterns and tendencies of the subtypes vary depending on which of the three survival instincts dominates your experience.

Self-Preservation 9 Subtype

This subtype merges with comfortable routines and physical activities like eating, reading, watching television, or doing puzzles. They tend to be more practical, grounded, concrete, irritable, and stubborn than the other two Type 9 subtypes. They are the hardest to move and like being alone more. They often have a good sense of humor.

Social 9 Subtype

This subtype devotes a great deal of time and energy to supporting groups of different kinds. They work very hard and tend to be more hardworking than any other type except Type 3. However, they usually don't show their stress. They tend to be good mediators and make great leaders, because they tend to be modest and try to be of service to others. They often don't feel as if they belong, no matter how hard they work. They experience sadness beneath the surface as a result.

Sexual (One-to-One) 9 Subtype

This subtype merges the most completely with important individuals. They may take on feelings, opinions, and attitudes from others and not experience a sense of boundaries with them. They tend to be the sweetest, most shy, and most emotional of the three subtypes, as well as the least assertive. They may not have a sense of their own purpose and may take on a purpose from others without realizing it. They often don't put themselves in the picture.

The Type 9 Subtype Shadows

You can more effectively recognize and own your specific Shadow aspects if you know the specific shadow characteristics of your Type 9 subtype. Below are some of the shadow characteristics of each subtype. As subtype behaviors can be highly automatic and unconscious, these traits may be the hardest to see and own.

Self-Preservation 9 Shadow

It will be important for you to notice if you tend to get stubborn and display other passive-aggressive behaviors when you feel disrespected or pressured by others. You may dig your heels in and refuse to move in reaction to being told what to do. You may "go to sleep" to your own anger and power and avoid any consciousness of anger as a way to stay safe and comfortable. You may not always see when your anger leaks out as stubbornness. You may tend to lose yourself in comfortable activities and routines as a way to avoid showing up in the world and expressing strong opinions, taking a stand, asserting power, or initiating change. You will need to become aware of your anger and own your power to grow.

Social 9 Shadow

Notice if work too hard to avoid feeling sad when you do not feel included in the group. Notice how you lose yourself in activity and service to others as a way to narcotize ("go to sleep to") your pain. You may sacrifice yourself to provide the group (or family) with humble leadership. You tend to be friendly and positive to avoid feeling or expressing anger. Notice if you mediate conflicts and support group cohesion to avoid feeling the discomfort of disharmony. Be more aware of how you focus on reducing tension in your environment so you don't have to confront the ways in which you may disagree with others. It will be good for your growth if you can be more opinionated and stir up some controversy.

Sexual (One-to-One) 9 Shadow

Notice how you merge completely with specific people in your life, to the point of erasing yourself. Be more aware of how you lack boundaries without being aware of the consequences of this. You may tend to have difficulty saying what you really think to people. Notice if you often stay silent or express agreement automatically, saying only what others want to hear or feeling opposition in secret. You may be unclear about your own sense of purpose and unsure of what you really want. You will need to get in touch with and act on your own individual desires and sense of purpose to further your growth.

. . . .
"If you don't like something, change it. If you can't change it, change your attitude." —Maya Angelou
. . . .

The Type 9 Paradox

The Type 9 paradox is grounded in the polarity between the passion of sloth and the virtue of right action. For this type, becoming more aware of their tendency to stay comfortably invisible and not bring their gifts to the world is how they begin to wake up. By becoming more aware of how sloth operates in their lives, they move away from their tendency to erase themselves and work toward expressing their power. For this type, being in right action means waking up to how important they are and learning to assert their own priorities.

The virtue of right action is a state of feeling powerfully motivated to do exactly the right thing at the moment it's needed. It is a wisdom of the heart that allows this type to identify and engage with exactly what needs to be done. It implies owning their own power to make important things happen and feeling worthy of receiving what they need. When Type 9s are in touch with right action, they can quickly and accurately spot the highest-priority task and won't stop until they get it done. Right action makes them stop putting off things that support their own being in the world. It makes them aware of their tendency to "go to sleep" to themselves and encourages them to become motivated to wake up and take care of their own needs.

If you identify as a Type 9, here are some steps you can take to become more conscious of your sloth and and access the higher-level state of right action:

- Begin acting on your own behalf and develop the ability to execute exactly what you need to do to support yourself and your process of awakening.

- Catch yourself in the act of minimizing yourself without judging yourself for it. Ask yourself why you repeatedly make yourself unimportant.

- Have compassion for yourself when you don't know what you want, especially if you get frustrated with yourself. Be upset with the habitual pattern, instead of with yourself. Give yourself time to discover more about your preferences. Know that this is a process that will get better over time if you work at it.

- Notice how sensitive you get when others make you unimportant. Then notice that you also do this to yourself—and how you do it. Remember why you are important and what the world will miss if you continue to forget yourself.

- Recognize that your tendency to want to include everyone is a projection of your desire to be heard and not excluded. Learn to speak up—to say what you think in the moment.

- Observe how you lose energy when it's time for you to do something important for yourself. Notice how you distract yourself or get uncomfortable or unclear when you need to act to support yourself. Try to stay connected to the reasons behind what you need to do for yourself.

- -

"The best politics is right action." —Mahatma Gandhi

- -

Using Type 9 Arrow Lines for Growth

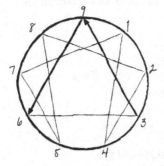

The two personality types connected to Type 9 by the arrow lines within the Enneagram diagram are Types 3 and 6. This type can create big growth movements to break away from their need to maintain harmony and comfort by concentrating more on setting and achieving bold goals the way healthy Type 3s do. They can create more inner balance by integrating Type 3's ability to self-promote and take credit for successes, and then developing Type 6's capacity to disagree and go against others.

- First, adopt Type 3s' ability to create a clear agenda and get focused on doing all the tasks you need to do to achieve a specific result. Develop more comfort being the center of attention. Own your strengths. Allow yourself to be recognized by others for the things you do well. Practice speaking up and taking the credit when you accomplish something. Speak in a clear, more concise, bottom-line way. Put yourself out there in a professional way. Care more about your image and take action to look good. Work to overcome your resistance to showing off and promoting yourself.

- Then integrate the Type 6 ability to think more proactively about how to accomplish things that may be dangerous or risky. Express more assertiveness by saying what you think and "going against" something. Communicate clearly and directly when you disagree with others. Overcome your tendency to keep smiling, even when you don't plan to do what others want you to do. Practice "poking holes" in someone's plan, raising a different opinion, or promoting a controversial, contrarian idea in a group. Learn to say "no" and point out why something won't work. Rebel against authority for a good cause. Get more in touch with any fears you have and take action in specific ways despite them. Recognize your self-doubt—but own your power and be more confident.

"A comfort zone is a beautiful place, but nothing
ever grows there." —John Assaraf

EMBRACING THE HIGH SIDE

On the third part of their journey, this type begins to focus more on their own needs and starts to connect more regularly and deeply with their internal experience. By consciously working to "remember themselves," they come to understand their blind spots and face their pain and their anger. They realize the full measure of their power and begin to gather back all the energy they dispersed outside themselves when they focused only on supporting others and meeting external demands.

If you are a Type 9, here are some things you can do at this stage of your journey that you couldn't do before—and what you can continue to work on:

- Take the most important actions to transform projects, yourself, and others, even if it involves confrontation or disruption. Be guided by your heart.

- Draw on a much bigger amount of energy (or life force) than you had before—with the clear recognition that this is the "real you."

- Be the leader the world has been waiting for. Actively balance an inclusive approach with an ability to discern and act on the wisdom of the best of differing perspectives.

- Inspire confidence and trust in others by personifying power and decisiveness mixed with modesty, thoughtfulness, and selfless service.

- Tolerate conflict with the clear understanding that the best connections are achieved by working through challenges and discord together.

- Value your own opinions, agenda, and vision as much as you respect and support those of others. Develop clarity about what you think and want.

- Be assertive and strong in order to activate and support the best in others without taking yourself out of the equation.

- Work against the tendency to take refuge in resignation or indifference and open up to actively receiving the love you deserve.

- Be recognized for the contributions you make (that only you could have made), while feeling a deep connection to the collective.

> "I awoke, only to find that the rest of the world is still asleep." —Leonardo da Vinci

The Type 9 Virtue

Right action is the virtue that provides an antidote to the passion of sloth. When in touch with right action, this type resists giving way to others or putting others ahead of themselves. They realize that they don't have to be overly modest or forget themselves to have value and create harmony. They know how to make their specific contribution to the world by embracing their own importance and knowing that they belong. They initiate projects that can change the world, instead of just doing more of the same old operational, routine stuff.

When Type 9s move into a state of right action, they learn to express their unique individuality, even while experiencing a deeper sense of connectedness to everything around them. They learn to bear discomfort and develop the ability to stay awake and energized by tapping into their own energy and channeling it more consciously in support of their own agendas. They take better care of themselves and express themselves more actively and powerfully in the world. They become leaders who combine attention and care for others with a clear sense of purpose based on the inner truth of who they are. This inner truth is characterized by a sense of self-remembrance and personal power. They experience their fully enlivened selves from the inside. They know what they want and they speak it clearly for the benefit of all. They understand that when they focus on manifesting their own desires, they may risk separation, but realize that this supports building true union in the long run.

In right action, the Type 9 heart knows its priorities. In this state, they feel an unstoppable willingness to make those things happen right now in the most effective way. They move effortlessly, yet with a lot of strength, toward those priorities and bring their energy—which is the biggest of all nine types—to the task. They know they are just as important as everybody else and have faith in their capacity to make things happen. They may sometimes feel a drive to disrupt things to help people and systems break away from the old and bring in what's new and necessary. They feel compelled to focus on what matters most and undertake positive conflict.

If you are a Type 9, right action enables you to wake up to all the ways you get lazy about your priorities. It initiates a movement in your heart that draws from a deep sense of inner knowing—and creates a new capacity in you to act on what you want in an ongoing way, sparked by your own natural vitality. As you move toward right action, here are some of the things you will experience:

- Being fully present in your heart while also being connected to your body and your mind. Cultivating an active focus on being more awake, alive, and embodied in the here and now.

- Doing diligent inner work that counteracts the powerful pull of the habitual state of sleep. Doing everything it takes to overcome inertia and awaken to what's true for you.

- Waking up to your own agenda through a deepening awareness of (and frustration about) all the ways you stay asleep.

- Actively observing the ways in which you operate mechanically rather than in accord with your deepest desires.

- Feeling an unstoppable motivation driven by the inner wisdom of your heart.

- Feeling a deep connection to your own inner energy and your own sense of being—the energy and being of someone who is truly alive.

- Applying yourself to practices that expand your consciousness of your inner truth.

- Engaging effectively with yourself and the world around you.

"Right attitudes produce right action." —Fyodor Dostoyevsky

Waking Up from the Zombie State

For Type 9s, the key to embracing the true self lies in gradually learning to empower themselves. This can seem difficult, if not impossible, because when they exist as zombies, they find it hard to know what they want and to recognize their inner authority. It can be painful for them to delve into their own being and feel a sense of separation. When 9s fear that connecting with themselves means disconnecting from the world of others, they may resist knowing their true inner selves and understanding how important they are as exactly who they are. But by contacting their anger and their power, and learning to embody all the energy they habitually disperse trying to create harmony, they can move toward a liberating experience of the virtue of right action.

When 9s realize that their tendency to over-adapt to others to the point of erasing themselves doesn't really help anybody, they begin to focus all their attention on doing what they need to do. They learn that living for comfort yields few tangible rewards and see that it's better to weather some discomfort than to stay asleep. By accepting how important they are, they become capable of giving and receiving love in a way that allows them to increase true union in the world. And when they experience *real* peace and harmony—the kind that only comes through an acceptance of discomfort and conflict—they realize that their fear of separation was just a delusion and that their true selves are connected to everything in the deepest way possible. As they come to know their authentic selves, they gain access to a higher experience of unity—a state in which they belong to everyone and everything. But to achieve this unity, they first have to create some disruption.

When they courageously face their Shadow—and especially their avoidance of anger and the way this leads them to deny their own power—9s gain freedom from the deadening comfort of sleep. By accessing the power within, they take action to travel the path that leads to their own awakening. They discover and enact the wishes of their fully awakened selves. When they dedicate themselves to staying connected to the things they resist most—their pain, their discomfort, and their deeply felt desire for a fully enlivened experience of life—they provide an example for all of us of how to travel the path toward reanimation and self-remembrance.

Conclusion

Each of us has something to give that no one else has.

Elizabeth O'Connor

The Enneagram symbol has roots in ancient wisdom traditions. The teachings connected to it reveal the possibilities for human transformation. The knowledge it reveals confirms that inner work can help us achieve higher states of consciousness.

The transformation process mapped by the Enneagram does not end, however, with the third step of the growth path described in this book, and we hope you will feel motivated to continue your journey beyond what's found in these pages. To support you in this, we offer the following suggestions:

- Ask for help. Therapy with a professional you like and trust can be life-changing.

- Seek "friends on the path." Share what you've learned with a community of like-minded others who can support your efforts.

- Do research. Rely only on solid information to ensure that you keep moving forward in the most effective way.

- Don't judge yourself. Learn from any setbacks you experience, then stand up and move forward on your path. Self-criticism stops your forward momentum on your journey of self-development and serves no constructive purpose. Practice compassion for yourself and others.

As you continue your inner work, you will experience the peace and joy that come to sincere seekers. There will be challenges along the way, but these are merely opportunities to develop the resilience you need to get to where you want to go.

And don't fall into the trap of just "upgrading your ego." Remember that self-development aims for transcendence. If your orientation is spiritual, don't ignore the psychological aspects of growth. If your orientation is psychological, don't ignore the spiritual aspects. Psychology without spirituality is limited; spirituality without psychological work is dangerous.

We hope that the Enneagram helps you manifest your highest potential. We hope you are transformed by its insights and enjoy (or learn from) every step on your journey. And finally, we hope that you share your stories about awakening to your authentic self to inspire others to find and follow their own path.

Acknowledgments

Many people helped in the inspiration, emergence, and production of this book. We are grateful for Greg Brandenburgh of Hampton Roads Publishing for approaching us with the initial idea for this book—as well as for the good-humored way he shepherded the project through the publishing process. We would like to thank Amanda Braga for her production help and for our team of Amanda and Tatiana Vilela for all they did to manage Chestnut Paes Enneagram Academy (and CP Online) during the writing process. This book has been an outgrowth of our collaboration in creating this "inner work" school (and the content that supports it) that has been the main vehicle for getting our Enneagram work out there into the world.

We would also like to thank Nancy Hunterton for her wise counsel—she has been an invaluable consultant who has helped us to improve the ways we work together. And we are grateful to Denise Daniels for her friendship and enthusiastic support of this project and our work generally—and to Dan Siegel for agreeing to write the foreword introducing this book. We appreciate Dan and Denise and their collaborators on their own forthcoming book, Laura Baker, and our longtime friend, Jack Killen, for their encouragement and their ongoing work to ground the Enneagram framework in science.

Both of us received our early Enneagram training from David Daniels, MD and Helen Palmer through their Narrative Tradition School. Helen and David were important mentors and teachers for us, and we feel very thankful for the solid foundation of the Enneagram training and experience we received from them. Although we lost David two years ago, his wise and warm spirit continues to inspire and motivate us. We also want to acknowledge the work of G. I. Gurdjieff, Oscar Ichazo, and Claudio Naranjo, seminal authors of the modern Enneagram teaching, as our work draws on theirs in many ways—as well as our good friend and ally, Russ Hudson, for his steadfast support and his enormous contribution to furthering the true spirit behind the Enneagram as a growth tool.

Finally, we are grateful to our literary agent, Peter Steinberg, for being part of our team and supporting our efforts—and to our friends, students, and staff in the larger Enneagram community and the Chestnut Paes Academy community for being dedicated companions on the path of self-development. Together we will work to create a more conscious world.

About the Authors

Beatrice and Uranio have been friends and colleagues since 2002. They worked together on the board of directors of the International Enneagram Association from 2004 to 2009, each serving as president for two years. Guiding global thought leaders in Enneagram theory and applications, in 2018 they cofounded Chestnut Paes Enneagram Academy, an international Enneagram-based school dedicated to raising the level of human consciousness through providing opportunities to apply the Enneagram system in support of deep inner growth work. They specialize in offering self-development courses and inner-work retreats that help people achieve inner transformation, and high-quality professional workshops that support coaches, therapists, counselors, and leaders in learning to use the Enneagram skillfully, effectively, and ethically with their clients.

Through their CP Enneagram Academy, Beatrice and Uranio do work around the world using the Enneagram as a map, a process, and a catalyst for personal and professional transformation. They develop Enneagram theory, methods, and content, such as this book, to leverage Enneagram insights to help people make real progress on a clear path of evolution. To find out more, visit *www.cpenneagram.com* and consider becoming a member of our community.

BEATRICE CHESTNUT, PHD MA is a licensed psychotherapist, coach, and business consultant based in San Francisco. She has a PhD in communication studies and an MA in clinical psychology. A student of the Enneagram system for over thirty years and a certified Enneagram teacher in the Palmer/Daniels Narrative Tradition school, she is author of the books, *The Complete Enneagram: 27 Paths to Greater Self-Knowledge* and *The 9 Types of Leadership: Mastering the Art of People in the 21st-century Workplace.*

Uranio Paes, MM worked in corporate settings for over two decades as an Enneagram facilitator, coach, and organization development consultant. Also certified as an Enneagram teacher through the Palmer/Daniels Narrative Tradition school, for many years Uranio taught their Enneagram Professional Training Program (EPTP) in Brazil, Spain, Portugal, and Italy. For over twenty years he trained as a student in three different spiritual traditions where he engaged in a deep study of different forms of spiritual practice.

HAMPTON ROADS PUBLISHING COMPANY

...for the evolving human spirit

Hampton Roads Publishing Company publishes books on a variety of subjects, including spirituality, health, and other related topics.

For a copy of our latest trade catalog, call (978) 465-0504 or visit our distributor's website at *www.redwheelweiser.com.* You can also sign up for our newsletter and special offers by going to *www.redwheelweiser.com/newsletter/.*